ARCANUM 17

André Breton

Arcanum 17

with

APERTURES

Grafted to the End

Translated from the French by Zack Rogow
and with an Introduction by
Anna Balakian

SUN &
MOON

CLASSICS

51

LOS ANGELES
SUN & MOON PRESS
1994

Sun & Moon Press
A Program of The Contemporary Arts Educational Project, Inc.
a nonprofit corporation
6026 Wilshire Boulevard, Los Angeles, California 90036

This edition first published in paperback in 1994 by Sun & Moon Press
10 9 8 7 6 5 4 3 2 1
FIRST ENGLISH LANGUAGE EDITION
©1944, 1965 Société Nouvelle de Editions Pauvert
Published in French as *Arcane 17*
Reprinted by agreement with Editions Pauvert
English translation ©1994 by Zack Rogow
Translator's Preface ©1994 by Zack Rogow
Introduction ©1994 by Anna Balakian
All rights reserved

The translator wishes to thank Madame Elisa Breton for her words of encouragement;
Bill Zavatsky for being the first midwife of this book; Philippe Durant and Christophe
Wall-Romana for correcting the mistakes; Paul Hammond for his useful suggestions;
Edwige LeBlanc of the Association Touristique de la Gaspésie for providing information on
that region; and Dr. Allison V. Andors of the Department of Ornithology of the American
Museum of Natural History for his help in translating certain technical terms.

This book was made possible, in part, through an operational grant from the
Andrew W. Mellon Foundation and through contributions to
The Contemporary Arts Educational Project, Inc.,
a nonprofit corporation

Cover Concept: Katie Messborn
Cover Design: Shari Spier /Reactor Art + Design Limited (Toronto, Canada)
Typography: Guy Bennett

LIBRARY OF CONGRESS CATALOGING IN PUBLICATION DATA
Breton, André (1896-1966)
Arcanum 17 (Arcane 17)
p. cm — (Sun & Moon Classics: 52)
ISBN: 1-55713-170-8
I. Title. II. Series.
811'.54—dc20

Printed in the United States of America on acid-free paper.

Contents

Introduction

André Breton (1896 – 1966) is a major French poet for whom the distinction between verse and prose did not exist. According to him poetry is a state of mind that encompasses all writing resulting from the passionate embrace of all entities human, animal, plant, and mineral that constitute the network of this earth. His work consists of free verse, cadenced prose, and a new structure of writing, the analogical form of the current work, *Arcanum 17*.

After the heyday of Surrealism, of which he was the official founder, Breton had abandoned automatic writing and developed a new form of narrative in his successive works, *Nadja* (1927 – 8), *Les Vases communicants* (1931 – 2), and *L'Amour fou* (1937) in which image associations direct the course of the narrative; these images are harvested from conscious reality and the dream without arbitrary barriers separating the two states. The impact of dream on reality balances the impact of reality on dream to create a more complete awareness of reality. The manipulations of the forces of chance and probability became his major concern in creating a sequence for events. He was also moving away from the short poem to three long ones which I consider his epic vision. It is significant perhaps that he wrote his great poems in transit and self-imposed exile in America, away from the Paris cenacle of the Surrealists: *Fata Morgana* (written in Marseille in 1941), *Les Etats-Généraux* (written in New York in 1943) and *Ode à Charles Fourrier* (1947) inspired by his travels in the American Far West during the war years.

As a graduate student at Columbia University, I had visited him at his dreary walk-up apartment on West 11th Street in 1942 and found him looking more like a lion trapped in a cage than like the unbridled revolutionary of his earlier age. This poet had perhaps been the most influential catalyst in the development of modern painting, before whom had trembled Dali, Tanguy, Matta, Arshile Gorky and a host of others. After his return to France he was to collaborate in his final poetic work with Miró to recreate, in poetic language, the cosmic vision of Miró's *Constellations.* Yet he took a dim view of museums as traps for artists, and he kept his distance from the society of artists and their patrons in America. He was seeking in the loneliness of his exile a meaning, a direction; and hating masters, whether divine or political, ("Ni Dieu, ni Maître") found his final solace in primitive legend, and in alchemy, which seemed to provide powers for the mind to transform anguish into ecstasy. His most brilliant achievement in his physical and spiritual entrapment in America was indeed *Arcanum 17*.

In *Arcanum 17*, written during a three-month stay in Canada, on the Gaspé Peninsula, the self-exiled Frenchman tried to find light and hope in the bleakest year of World War II by seeking solace in the forces of the universe, the powers of love, the wisdom of old alchemical philosophies, particularly as transmitted by the defrocked nineteenth-century priest, Eliphas Lévi, (Abbé Constant), and ancient myths, as he confronted both the precarious quality of the human condition and the dire political situation of the time.

In writing *Arcanum 17* in the summer and fall of 1944, he must have thought of the Work in the alchemical sense of the word, the summit of all that preceded, as close to the top of his art and of his thought as he could reach. As the Great Work it was a synthesis of all that had gone before and as the amalgamation of all the elements that characterized him as a poet.

The title refers to the lore of the Hebraic-Bohemian-Egyptian tarot. In the cards of the tarot it is the seventeenth of the twenty-two, all of which are hieroglyphic in their representations; seventeen comes after fifteen and sixteen which are assigned to the work of the devil, in this instance war and darkness in human hearts. But after the fall of Lucifer suddenly the skies become luminous, and love and peace triumph through the intervention of the beautiful young woman who pours the contents of two urns upon the earth: containing love and intelligence. The seventeenth sign of the tarot is under the aegis of the Pentagram, the morning star.

To the wisdom of the old alchemists who ever tried to conciliate opposites in turning darkness into light, as the morning star in the heavens rising out of the black stratosphere, Breton adds the powers of a new love that had come into his life. After his wife, Jacqueline Lamba, had left him, taking along the little daughter whom he loved above all else, he had been "le veuf inconsolé" (the inconsolable widower) to borrow the words of Gérard de Nerval's mystical poem, "El Desdichado." To the grief of losing his wife is added the poignant lament of the parent who will miss the awakening of his child to the daily marvels of life; he will have no part in shaping that young, sparkling, open mind. But shortly before the voyage to Gaspé he had met by chance in a New York restaurant the Chilean Elisa, who had come back from her own Hades, having been twice through the shadow of the valley of death with deep personal losses.

It was under these tragic circumstances that he and Elisa set off on a *fugue* to one of the northern confines of the American continent, as close to the North Star and the North Pole as one who was ever fascinated by the North could hope to reach. They found a cabin in Sainte-Agathe at the tip of Gaspé near Percé Rock. He wrote every morning for three months, waking at five and writing until noon. Here is how in my critical biography of Breton I reconstructed the circumstances out of an interview given to me by Elisa shortly after the death of Breton, and out of Breton's own narrative text: "In the afternoons they would take walks, gather agate stones, visit the bird sanctuary of the island of Bonaventure where the resplendent array of birds seemed to Breton like a moving rainbow. They would watch the fishermen with their nets on the rugged coast of the Canadian peninsula, and the strata of sediments and erosions that spelled the history of the struggle of the soil against the water, wind, and sun. It was still the season of light, at five in the morning the air was luminous, and the sea had shed its night. The earth was in a constant state of metamorphosis as it now wrapped itself in mist, then shed it in triumph. To Breton this fluctuation, dramatic in its suddenness, was to seem like a curtain going up and coming down."[1]

1   *André Breton: Magus of Surrealism* (New York: Oxford University Press, 1971), p. 202.

Such were the conditions under which Breton wrote his last meditation on war, love, and resurrection. Like a symphony the work contains recurring themes and variations: the biographical, the mythological, and the ecological. In his analogical mind he combined the process of metamorphosis, basic to the alchemical philosophy, with the constant changes he observed in the natural appearance of the earth; the notion of reconstruction after destruction was identified in the image of the ancient black god Osiris who was destroyed and then brought back into being by the goddess Isis. His own new found love assumed an analogy with the medieval mythological figure of Melusina, the most French of fays, immortalized in Jean d'Arras's account of the fifteenth-century Poitou region, i.e. in the heart of France.

According to legend Melusina was one of the triplet daughters of Presine, a mysterious fay who married the powerful king of Albania. Melusina was doomed not to be totally human and had to return every Saturday night to the state of ondine—half woman, half water serpent. If Melusina married a mortal who had the endurance and willpower to abstain from looking at her on the day of her metamorphosis, she would bring him happiness and help him build a powerful empire. But if he succumbed to human curiosity she would lose her hold on mortality and become a creature of the water and the air, *but hover over her loved ones in time of impending peril and continue to protect them.* Through a random encounter, Melusina meets the Count of Poitiers, in an enchanting forest at a magic fountain, saves him from peril, marries him; but like Orpheus he fails to keep his promise and loses her to the elements. Yet she remains the protective force in his life and in establishing a dynasty.

The legend of Melusina is particularly appropriate because it supports Breton's haunting thought that man has unwittingly dislodged woman from a position where she could do much good for humanity. She is the symbol of the dispossessed—like Breton, like Elisa—"the woman deprived of her human dish." But beyond the personal analogy lies a far more important one that Breton proposed. Melusina represents womanhood itself which has been banished (this is in 1944) in modern civilization from a position of power for good to one of servitude. What Elisa has meant to him, is extended in Breton's mind to what woman in her total sense can mean to a world in jeopardy. He goes so far as to muse that the only salvation from the dire inhumanities in the world would be through the restoration of woman to a position similar to the one Melusina occupied for a brief legendary moment.

But Breton is no feminist in the political sense we use the word today. He is not asking for women's "equality" with men but something much greater. He is suggesting that woman is superior to man in the very resources that must be tapped to bring peace, harmony, and serenity on our planet. Intuitively like Melusina women are closer to nature, and thereby divine as only those beings who are wise in the intentions and mysteries of natural forces can be said to be divine. Here is how Breton words his thought: "This crisis is so severe that I, myself, see only one solution: the time has come to value the ideas of woman at the expense of those of man, whose bankruptcy is coming to pass fairly tumultuously today. It is artists, in particular, who must take the responsibility, if only to protest against this scandalous state of affairs, to maximize the importance of everything that stands out in the feminine world view in contrast to the masculine, to build only on woman's resources, to exalt, or even better to appropriate to

the point of jealously making it one's own, all that distin-
guishes her from man in terms of modes of appreciation and
volition." (p. 61)

The third set of analogies is identified with nature itself,
and principally with Percé Rock, which is erected by nature at
this septentrional limit of the continent, creating a barrier
that protects Breton and Elisa from "the insanity of the hour."
Septentrone pandetur omne malum (All misfortunes of the world
are written in the northern sky). Percé Rock, shutting out the
agony of Europe, gives Breton a poignant symbol of his isola-
tion, an anguished sense of guilt since he seems not to have
practiced what he had preached all his life, the active partici-
pation of the artist in the life of society. But there is the other
side of the coin in the analogy of Percé Rock: now it is there,
now it isn't. It disappears in the twilight, and in the morning
mist. But it is resplendent in the sun. It becomes a metaphor
for cosmic as well as human modifications. The Rock is com-
posed of geological strata, as civilization has its historical ep-
ochs superimposed one on the other. Breton's analogical eye,
with its habit of seeing one thing in another, merges the different
hues of the Rock equating the process with the soldering of
human cultures; he sees in the storms that batter the Rock
and leave in it their everlasting marks and endanger its resil-
ience, the bloodbaths of European wars and Europe's much
more rapid effacement. But the analogy of disintegration and
division suggested by the Rock's composition is compensated
by the image of unity and cohesion that its solid appearance
embodies, even as in the face of Europe's deconstruction and
fragmentation Breton insists on affirming the fundamental
unity and the oneness of humankind. "Civilization is one even
as this Rock." In making this declaration of faith at a time
when his world was collapsing he was sending out not a po-

litical message but a poetic one: that all the myths of the world concur to spell out in their hieroglyphics their stirring message that from darkness comes light, and that the only enemies of man are despair and resignation. He demonstrates through its multitudinous manifestations in the physical world that resurrection is not limited to religious belief but is a physical, material fact of life: the process of resurrection is as indestructible as the emergence of the morning star after the night. In one of his most poetic passages he identifies the link between the plant and the butterfly as the nonsupernatural evidence of resurrection: "before taking flight to attend to the dissemination of the fecundating substance, before finding again the stippled and sinuous line that directs its flight, it only seems to exist in order to bring to the attention of our eyes the sumptuousness of that wing. And in its turn it tells what a consoling mystery there is in the raising of successive generations, what new blood incessantly circulates and, so that the species may not suffer from the wearing down of the individual, what selection always takes place just in time, succeeds in imposing its law despite all. Man sees this trembling wing which is, in all languages, the capital letter that begins the word Resurrection." (p. 78)

Could Breton in 1944 still be viewed as the chief spokesman of the surrealist movement? Certainly the brazen manifestations of social and political revolt had disappeared. The poet had triumphed over the pamphleteer. In *Arcanum 17* there were still attacks on institutions: school, family, church, barracks, bank, factory. But as in the rest of his *poetic* writings, he avoided circumstantial polemics rampant in an atmosphere charged with political circumstances. Rebellion, personified here in a sympathetic vision of Lucifer, attempts to rise above the specifics of existing conditions but is centralized in the freedom of the imagination, of the human spirit to overcome particular obstacles. When his contemporaries like Sartre, Camus, and Anouilh were in the thick of things and pronouncing somber, existential attitudes at a time particularly appropriate for writings on the theme of *De profundis clamavi*, Breton was singing a hymn to life: in the eyes of a woman, in the austerity of a rock, in the grace of a butterfly he read the eternal values that cannot vanish, when all else vanishes, because they signal each in its own way that death is passing, and that in spite of the efforts of the human race to annihilate itself, life is indestructible.

This was a work that could understandably be derided at the time it was written. "You, who abandoned Europe in its peril, who are you to preach to us from the most secluded bastion of North America," was a general attitude, which was insinuated in the major literary circles in Paris after Breton's return to Paris at the end of the war. The sky that the newly rising generation of existentialists had declared null and void had become for Breton a fresh canvas on which to project his "signe ascendant" that he had refused to give up in spite of all the calamities.

Arcanum 17 in its unconventional structure and unpopular politics, did not have an impact in the world of letters at the time it was written. The Western world has not been in a mood to adopt a utopian philosophy in the last fifty years. It is probably the last of Breton's major works to be translated into English, happily so since it seems to have waited for Zack Rogow who has succeeded in preserving the voice of Breton, its variations from the lyric to the thunderous and its labyrinthine ways of winding into the sources of meaning.

But the fact remains that at the fiftieth anniversary of *Arcanum 17*, many of André Breton's predictions have come true. Long before anyone else he foresaw the impossibility of the survival of Marxism in the guise of the Soviet Union. He envisaged the possibilities of directing the theory of chaos to new channels in literature before it had a serious grip in the sciences. He probed the nature of human sexuality and the importance of woman power although not in the terms feminists have pursued. He made one of the most acerbic criticisms about the politically biased and morally narrow education system of the West. He would be the darling of the ecologists if they knew about him and read *Arcanum 17* in his perception of the intricate relationships that create the cohesion of the universe. Most readers today would approve the parallel he tried to show between the monistic fusion he discovered in nature and the need for the unity of Europe and the necessity, in fact, for humankind, deprived of its belief in anthropocentrism, to seek the solidarity of its planet.

Anna Balakian

Translator's Preface

Arcanum 17 breaks through the fences of traditional literary categories. Its language is part prose, part poetry. At times it reads like a love letter. In other passages it's more of a travel journal, a political pamphlet, a sampler of mythology and folk tales, or a meditation on the nature of poetry. Remarkably, these pieces form a unified suite of passages despite their variety of subjects and moods, and despite Breton dividing them into sections separated by pauses.

Arcanum 17 coheres because there is an idea that winds through all the different fields André Breton enters in the book. Breton finds this theme in nature, in his personal life, in mythology, and in the state of Western Europe at the turning point of World War II.

Breton wrote *Arcanum 17* during a trip to Quebec in the months after D-Day in 1944, when the Allied armies were liberating city after city following years of Nazi occupation. Breton had fled the German Occupation three years earlier, settling in New York for the duration of the War.

In New York Breton experienced the personal loss he alludes to in *Arcanum 17*. His second wife left him, taking with her their one child, an eight year-old daughter. But not long before he wrote *Arcanum 17*, Breton fell in love again, this time with the woman who became his third wife, Elisa. Elisa had also lost a mate through divorce and had suffered the loss by drowning of a teenaged daughter, her only child. Amidst the rubble of their lives, André and Elisa found the love of their lives. This paradox, discovering and appreciating love because of loss, is the heart of *Arcanum 17*.

Breton saw this twist in his personal life reflected in the political situation of his day. Europe was bleeding under the Nazi Occupation and the almost limitless violence of the War. But Breton hoped that the War had shocked France out of its complacency. The Occupation had given birth to the Resistance, and the Resistance had poured fuel on the fire that had been flickering in the decades before the War. Breton expresses the wish in *Arcanum 17* that the loss of liberty under the Occupation would result in a new understanding in the postwar period of the need for a dynamic and ever-changing form of freedom.

Even in the Quebec landscape Breton saw the pattern of appreciation through loss. He and Elisa stayed near Percé Rock, a gigantic slab in the Atlantic, abutting the Gaspé Peninsula. It wasn't the permanence of this immense rock that awed Breton. Just the opposite. Its impermanence, its slow-motion crumbling, was what moved him. Some of the most memorable passages in *Arcanum 17* occur in the section where Breton sees in the bird sanctuary of Quebec's Bonaventure Island a living diagram of Western culture at its most vital moments. In Quebec, Breton also discovered a home-grown surrealism not only in the figures suggested by Percé Rock and the stones he found on the beach, but in the unique idioms and folklore of Quebec, isolated for centuries from its European origins.

Breton felt his ideas were also embodied in the supernatural landscape of myths, folk tales, and the occult. He incorporates into the book the legend of the Egyptian god Osiris, who was resurrected by his sister-wife, Isis, after his brother murdered and mutilated him. Osiris' story provides a model of the triumph over suffering, a model Breton applies to personal and political tragedy.

Another myth Breton frequently mentions in *Arcanum 17* is a French folk tale about Melusina, the fairy who is said to watch over the Chateau of Lusignan. According to the legend, Melusina was human above the waist and serpentine below the waist for one day a week. She was doomed to lead a semi-human existence forever when her husband could not resist looking at her in her half-serpentine form. Her scream marked her return to a less than human world.[1] Breton uses Melusina as a symbol of the status of women in contemporary society—reduced to half her humanity because she cannot play a full role in our culture, yet because of this, "in providential communication with nature's elemental forces." He makes a strong case that the kind of pain caused by World War II will only end when women assume leadership. Readers of A.S. Byatt's novel, *Possession*, which also touches on the Melusina legend, will see that she owes quite a debt to Breton's feminist interpretation of this story.

Breton's feminism in *Arcanum 17* is the most striking fea-

---

[1] For a full elucidation of this myth and Breton's use of it, see *André Breton: Magus of Surrealism* by Anna Balakian (New York: Oxford University Press, 1971), pp. 203-5.

ture of the book because it seems so strong and far-sighted. Even today, this passage sounds revolutionary:

> ...those of us in the arts must pronounce ourselves unequivocally against man and for woman, bring man down from a position of power which, it has been sufficiently demonstrated, he has misused, restore this power to the hands of woman, dismiss all of man's pleas so long as woman has not yet succeeded in taking back her fair share of that power, not only in art but in life.

But in her book, *Women Artists and the Surrealist Movement*, the art historian Whitney Chadwick questions the depth of Breton's feminism in *Arcanum 17*. Criticizing the Surrealists, she writes:

> What they give us, finally, is not a role for women independent of man, even as they acknowledge her power and her proximity to the sources of creation, but a new image of the couple in which woman completes man, is brought to life by him, and, in turn, inspires him.[2]

Professor Chadwick makes a good point when she chides Breton for choosing the "child-woman" as his image of woman at her most powerful. This archetype, isolated from others, does infantilize women. But we should be careful when mea-

---

2   Whitney Chadwick, *Women Artists and the Surrealist Movement* (Boston: Little, Brown, and Co., 1985), p. 65.

suring the politics of a book written in 1944 by today's standards. For its time, *Arcanum 17* was explosive.

The title of *Arcanum 17* derives both from Breton's interest in feminism and from his fascination with the occult. Arcanum 17 is a card called The Star in the tarot deck. It's the seventeenth card in the Major Arcana, the section of the deck most charged with meaning. This card, which Breton describes in detail at one point in the book, depicts a sky of stars over the head of a naked woman, who is pouring water from two urns, one emptying into a pool and the other onto land. To fortune tellers this card represents hope, renewal, and resurrection, themes which saturate Breton's book. From a more hermetic standpoint, The Star portrays the channeling of superlunary forces into the mundane world. And it is a woman who is the medium of this transfer. The woman in this tarot card has, for Breton, a power similar to the one he ascribes to Melusina, Elisa, Isis, and the many other female figures he mentions in the book.

While Breton stuck to the position on feminism he espouses in *Arcanum 17*, he had second thoughts about what he'd written on war and nationalism.

To clarify his thinking on these issues he added a series of texts to the end of *Arcanum 17* when it was reprinted in 1947. These texts, gathered under the heading *Apertures*, are as prophetic as *Arcanum 17*.

In *Apertures* Breton argues for pacifism, without calling it by name. This pacifism surprises, not because Breton ever tried to rationalize any war, but because his youthful declarations had a recklessness and a touch of hostility that advocated violence. The experience of a second world war, though, seems to have smoothed that edge in Breton.

Breton warns that World War II was not an isolated phenomenon but a symptom of a cancer madly reproducing itself in our society. Of the extreme chauvinism and aggressiveness that developed in Germany under the Nazis, Breton asks, "Is it true, or rather will it be certain tomorrow that this error is particularly, exclusively German?" Nazism should not be equated with any other historical event, but now that we have witnessed the French war in Algeria, the U.S. in Vietnam, and the Russian invasions of Eastern Europe, we see how much sharper Breton's eyesight was than many of his contemporaries.

Breton advocated a new internationalism as a way of preventing war. In this he was decades ahead of Jonathan Schell, who made a similar call in his well-known essay, *The Fate of the Earth*. Breton goes beyond mere internationalism, however, to maintain that a fundamental shaking of daily life is a necessary precondition for eliminating war.

Breton's thinking in *Arcanum 17* and *Apertures* is *not* the Marxist-Leninism dominant among intellectuals of his generation, despite his fling with the Communist Party and his friendship with Trotsky. Though written in the 1940s, this book is inspired by a free-spirited radicalism which prefigures the politics of the 1960s. Breton died in the fall of 1966. Just a year and a half later, France erupted in a general strike that featured slogans curiously close to Breton's ideas, such as L'IMAGINATION AU POUVOIR (POWER TO THE IMAGINATION). There is a saying in France—*"André Breton a raté sa fête;"*—"André Breton missed his own party."

San Francisco, California: 1994

ARCANUM 17

I N ELISA'S DREAM that old gypsy woman who was try-
ing to kiss me while I ran away, but that was Bonaventure
Island, one of the largest aquatic bird sanctuaries in the
world. We had visited it that same morning under an overcast
sky, on a fishing boat in full sail and had enjoyed at the begin-
ning, the arrangement, completely random, but in the style of
Hogarth, of the floats made of yellow or red casks, whose
lower portions were painted with cabalistic looking signs, casks
topped by long poles which ended in waving black flags (the
dream no doubt seized on these devices, grouped in irregular
bunches on the deck, to dress the gypsy). The smacking of the
flags stayed with us the whole way until about the time that
our attention was caught by the sight, defying the imagina-
tion, of the abrupt wall of the island, step after step fringed
with a foam of living snow and endlessly reworked with wide
and whimsical scrapes of a blue trowel. Personally, I found the
scene gripping: for a good quarter of an hour my thoughts
just wanted to be white oats in that thresher. Sometimes a

nearby wing, ten times longer than its counterpart, consented to spell out a letter, never the same one, but I was immediately taken with the extravagant character of the whole inscription. The word symphony has been used with regard to the rocky ensemble that dominates Percé, but here was an image which only became powerful from the moment one discovered that the repose of the birds was a perfect match for the craggy shapes of those sheer battlements, so that the organic rhythm was perfectly superimposed on the inorganic rhythm, as if it needed to fuse with it in order to hold itself together. Who could have thought of lending the elasticity of wings to an avalanche? The different rock beds, slipping with one supple line from the horizontal to the oblique at a forty-five degree angle to the water, are delineated by a marvelous chalk mark, constantly agitated (I'm daydreaming of a turned-down bed-spread of the same color white, in fine lace, whose large flowers fascinated me on waking when I was a child). It's marvelous that the very folds imprinted on the rock beds by the ages create a trampoline for what is most inviting about life: the soaring, the just-veering-off, and the luxurious drifting of aquatic birds. There's a star that quivers above all that seeks, and then immediately and ferociously avoids human contact, like very little girls (recently the eleven-month old of my friends Arshile and Agnès Gorky, so purely magical, turning her shoulder away and looking very offended when I made as if to take her hand and bring her back, her eyes ever brighter, begging with all the power of playfulness and grace for what she was fleeing) or like the minks, some brown, some white, which we surprised not far from here on a farm—when we walked past a row of their cages, they quickly ran and huddled under cover when we passed by, but came out and moved up close to look us over as we walked away. Poetic thought, of course, shares a great affinity with this way of behaving. It's the enemy of patina and it's perpetually on guard against all that is burning to seize it: this is what distinguishes it, in essence, from ordinary thought. To remain what it must be, a conductor of mental electricity, it must, above all, undertake its task in an *isolated* setting.

Isolation, on this Gaspé coast, is as unexpected today and as complete as can be. This region of Canada lives, in effect, under its own laws and in spite of everything, somewhat at the margins of history, because it is incorporated into an English dominion but has kept not only France's language, in which all sorts of anachronisms have taken up residence, but also the deep impression of its customs. Perhaps, dramatic as it is, the current landing of numerous French Canadians on the Normandy coast will help reestablish a vital link, missing for almost two centuries. But those who have remained here indicate with their gestures and their remarks that they have never completely been able to get past the stage where their group identity blurs to merge with another. If, on their part, all rancor has probably disappeared, their integration into the heart of the English community appears altogether illusory. The Catholic church, true to its obscurantist methods, makes use here of its all-powerful influence to prevent the dissemination of any literature which is not edifying (classical theater has practically been reduced to *Esther* and *Polyeucte*, which are available in huge stacks in Quebec bookstores, the eighteenth century seems never to have taken place, Hugo is nowhere to be found). *Chariots*, as they call buses here, rare and wheezy, only regain a bit of confidence when they cross the *covered bridges* of a bygone era. What's more, this season has not been favorable for tourism. With very few exceptions, the Americans have refrained from coming for several years. The recent provincial elections, in which the reins of power passed from the Liberal Party to the Union National, will bring in their wake the redistribution of all public offices and dissuade both those already entrenched and those hoping to succeed them from making any vacation plans. The local newspapers, which report European news in a gleefully apocalyptic style, abound in information whose very presentation right in the middle of the page creates a dissonant effect ("For twenty-five consecutive nights veritable showers of meteors will light up the August sky"), alternating with recipes of a sibylline quality ("rolls of cornflowers": but these words only disguise a blueberry pie). All this creates, in the admirably limpid air, a very effective shield against the madness of the moment, like the mist which on certain mornings stretches from one end of the horizon to the other ("Alouette, natural smoking tobacco," frankly states this package with a picture of a bird singing in the grass and, with the first lines of a song that it tramples, all of Nerval's old Valois gushes out only to evaporate suddenly: *"Alouette, gentille alouette—Alouette, je te fumerai."*)

Suddenly the curtain fell on the bird colony which extends across only one part of the northeast shore of the island. My eyes couldn't find the puffin then but a *gannet* came and hovered close by, I had time to admire its saffron head, its doubly emerald eye between two junctions of its white wings fringed with black (the gannet is the bird which dominates Bonaventure Rock, where its kind is represented by six or seven thousand individuals. In contrast to the seagull with its pearl gray wings and the crested cormorant, it doesn't appear on the shores of Percé to take part in the gutting of the cod when the fishing boats bring in the catch). But we had doubled a cape: it was all over, not only for the phantasmagorical embroidery thrown over that immense red and black chest with blue locks barely issuant from the sea, but also for the orchestration which is inseparable from it and which one of our travelling companions said could best be compared to the sounds one hears above Fez. Once again only the whipping of flags at night. Eyes close, as after a blinding glare. What road is this whipping on? Where is the coachman travelling so late at night, maybe drunk, and apparently without even a lantern? It's true that the wind may have blown it out. I've never seen such a storm in all my life! And the imaginary team is swallowed up by a fault as it opens, ever widening along the flank of the rock and, in a flash, it uncovers the tortured heart of old Europe feeding the long trails of spilled blood. Somber Europe, just for a moment so far away. The vast red and rust clots are now forming right in front of my eyes with stains of excremental gold among cascades of blue gun barrels and propellers. Soiling it all, there are even vast splashes of ink as if to testify that a certain kind of writing, apparently quite common, is nothing more than a deadly venom, a virus that stirs up all evil... And yet beneath this veil of ominous significance an entirely different one rises with the sun. All these ridges arranging themselves, this whole assortment of geological beds rolled into plateaus and interrupted by tiers, these abrupt saggings, these smooth stretches sometimes beyond expectation, these zones from pink to purple that balance others from periwinkle to ultramarine by means of transversal beaches gradually becoming nocturnal and fiery, are the most fitting symbol for the structure of the edifice of human culture in the narrow intrication of the parts that make it up, defying all impulses to remove any one of them. Under this movable earth—the soil of that rock crowned with fir trees—runs a subtle thread that can't be broken and that connects the peaks and some of those peaks are a certain fifteenth century in Venice or Sienna, an Elizabethan sixteenth, a French second half of the eighteenth, a German Romantic beginning of the nineteenth, a Russian corner of the twentieth. No matter what passions may seem to deny this evidence in our time, the entire foreseeable future of the human spirit rests on this complex and indivisible substratum. It will be quite another task to prevent, if the desire is real, the return of catastrophes analogous to the one which is ending by eliminating antagonisms on a different scale; but any wish to humiliate in this area for the purpose of retaliation could only serve to impoverish the humiliator. One might as well try to plunder oneself. Civilization, independent of the not unsolvable conflicts of interest which undermine it, is *one*, like this rock on whose summit sits man's home (from the beach at Percé only one can be made out at night, from a luminous dot flickering on the water). Who is he? Doesn't matter. In this luminous dot is concentrated all that life holds in common.

Gathered above our heads, the pennants of forever darkened windows continued to lap up their share of the air. They were the same size as the red canvas ones that flank certain road construction projects in Paris and on which stand out in large black letters separated by periods, the inscription "SADE," often riveting my daydreams. I will always see the red flag, free of marks or symbols, through the eyes I had when I was seventeen years old, when, during a worker's demonstration as the last war drew near, I saw it unfurled by the thousands under the low sky of the Pré Saint-Gervais. And yet—I sense that reason won't help at all with this—I will continue to tremble even more at the memory of the moment when that blazing sea—in a few very limited areas—was pierced by black flags taking wing. I was not yet very aware politically and I really have to admit that I'm still perplexed when I try to gauge how it changed me. But more than ever, currents of sympathy and antipathy seem to me strong enough to bend ideas and I know that my heart did beat, will continue to beat with the very rhythm of that day. In the deepest levels of my heart, I will always find the play of those countless tongues of fire, some of which linger to lick a superb, charred flower. Younger generations can hardly understand a spectacle like the one back then. All sorts of lacerations at the heart of the working class had not yet come to pass. The torch of the Paris Commune was far from having gone out, there were many hands there which had held it, it united everything with its great light which would have been less beautiful, less true, without a few plumes of thick smoke. So much unselfish faith, so much determination and fervor could be read in those faces, and so much nobility in those of the old people. Around the black flags, certainly the physical devastation was more palpable, but passion had truly drilled some of those eyes, had left dots of unforgettable incandescence. In any case, it was as if the flame had swept over all of them, only partly burning them, fostering in some of them only the most reasonable, the best founded hopes and demands; while it led the others, though fewer, to consume themselves on the spot with an inexorable attitude of sedition and defiance. The human condition is such that, independent of the utterly rectifiable social conditions that man has created for himself, this latter attitude, for which, in intellectual history, there is no lack of guarantors, be they Pascal, Nietzsche, Strindberg, or Rimbaud, has always seemed to me the most justifiable from an emotional point of view, putting aside the completely utilitarian reasons society has for repressing it. At least one has to recognize, despite oneself, that it alone is marked by a diabolical grandeur. I will never forget the relief, the exaltation, and the pride aroused, one of the very first times as a child I was taken to a cemetery—among so many depressing or ridiculous funerary monuments—by the discovery of a simple slab of granite carved in red capitals with the superb motto: NEITHER GOD NOR MASTER. Poetry and art will always have a weakness for all that transfigures man in that hopeless appeal, indomitable, which now and then he takes the laughable risk of issuing to life. The fact is that above art, above poetry, like it or not, a flag alternately red and black is waving. There again, time is running short: it's a matter of returning to the human heart all that it can give out. But where does that seeming ambiguity come from, that final indecision regarding the color? Perhaps a particular man may act on the hearts of other men in order to mold them, to expand them, only on the condition that he sacrifice himself to all the scattered powers in the soul of his era, which, in general, only seek each other out in order to exclude one another. It's in this sense that this man is, that he always has been, and that, by a mysterious decree of those powers, he *must* be at the same time their victim and their master. The same holds true true for a certain taste for human liberty which, called to widen the field of universal receptivity even minutely, brings down on a solitary being all the fatal consequences of immoderation. Liberty consents to caress the earth a little, if only for the sake of those who have not known or who have barely known how to live, having loved it *madly*... But we will let some go back to their garrets in Charonne or Malakoff, others resume telling the same old jokes in the bistros. What beautiful lines with a hundred brand new fishhooks, there, all in a row. The flags won't take us any farther: the launch is coming to bring us back to solid ground.

Even while enjoying the present moment as much as possible, I can't completely overcome the worry penetrating the depths of my soul. My privileged position, at this very instant, reinforces in me, by contrast, my awareness of the partiality of the fate which dooms so many over there to terror, to hatred, to slaughter, to famine. This period is so harsh that one hardly dares declare these things, ashamed of looking as though one wants to parade one's lovely sentiments. One of the worst effects of the ethics of war erupts when, truly proscribing these sentiments as soft, it succeeds in making them appear suspect, or at least seriously out of place. The state of mind which results from this will become more defensive than ever on the day when it's reported that the Allied armies have reached the gates of Paris. What can I do about it, the sense of an even greater unevenness takes hold of me and I accept it as justifiable in the only world that's important to me, the world cured of its fury. No, despite certain indications, all has not yet been sacrificed to the military Moloch. How often, first in France, then in America, I've observed with relief, what am I saying, with a joy so completely comforting, behind the scenes of this war: never has poetry—I'm not speaking of occasional poetry—been so enthusiastically devoured. It even seems as if countless ears have opened to it which otherwise would have remained deaf. It is easy to see in this phenomenon the manifestation of that need to take a *detour through the essential,* such as one experiences each time there's a threat to one's individual existence or even to the pursuit of one's personal destiny within the framework of that existence. I maintain that when the nature of events tends to head them in a direction that is too painful, people's feelings find, despite themselves, a refuge and a springboard in the most perfect expressions of what is not real, I mean those where a completely different "reality" has been able to make the eternal, until reabsorbed in the distance, spring forth. How was it translated in its highest form, on that morning at sea, that mixture of joy and apprehension stirred by the immediate fate of Paris, and made up of my approaching and leaving Bonaventure Rock and its birds? It was translated in language much imbued with stanzas of Baudelaire. And it wasn't I reciting them.

Calamity is so great, so all-engrossing when one is in it that few try to find a parallel for it in history, which might, however, give birth to some new hope: "Paris is no longer a stage for tender and joyful scenes: no one there has a joke at the ready; everyone there is preoccupied with his own sorrows and misery." The work that I'm borrowing this quotation from takes off its gloves to judge the behavior of the Head of State: "He concentrates and expends what energy and vitality remain to him with the short and painful efforts of an old man, in little senile movements, in the indulgence of fleeting and uncouth whims... Human rag who shrivels and freezes, he continues to live out his normal daily life with a frightening punctuality... He is living his last winter in the anguish of his chateau, where they treated themselves to a New Year's Day gift of a few sticks of wood, as if they were jewels." The subject here is not recent conditions in France, this was its condition during the last year of the reign of Louis XIV, but what the author, Virgile Josz, according to Saint-Simon and others, goes on to report about the deplorable behavior of most of the great men and about the repugnant intrigues woven in the Court leaves us no choice but to try to draw the parallel. What holds the interest of the writer I just referred to is not the overwhelming horror, but actually the project of helping to reveal on that dark canvas a glow kindled in the human spirit to vanquish that horror, it's the star that makes you forget the mud, it's Watteau's angelic personality. Watteau's work has, in fact, the value of forcing us by its glory to exorcise all that can be crushing about the egotism and nastiness of men in periods of setback. Even though deliverance from the regime under which Watteau suffered was so long delayed, the anguish and turpitude of his time are no longer crucial to us, yet he's the one who continues to reign over our emotions. Better still, we are led more and more to see that whole atrocious epoch through his dreams. If he touches on the military pomp of those bygone days: those three-cornered hats, those bandoliers, those coat-tails, he only sings what twinkles in the eyes of girls and makes them show off the suppleness of their waists, the bounce of their busts. He keeps us far from the throes of battle: the struggle only takes on the dimensions of the eternal tournament of love, although the beauties do not resist.

These hardships, these sorrows which early on destroy his health, it's marvelous to see them completely absorbed into a hymn to the one and only glory of nature and love. So every storm, with the advent of a beautiful day, manages to be swallowed up and negate itself in a pearl. Under that adorable foliage, too widespread and too vivacious to suffer from the quarrels of men, everything tends, *must tend* in the final analysis, toward a reorientation of what can be deduced from life.

A woman's hand, your hand in its starry paleness only to help you walk downstairs, refracts its beam into my own. Its slightest touch branches out inside me and in a moment will trace above us those delicate canopies where the inverted sky stirs its blue leaves with misty aspen or willow. As for me, to what do I actually owe this remission of a pain that so many others suffer because of less guilt than I feel today? Before I met you I'd known misfortune, despair. Before I met you, come on, those words mean nothing. You know very well that when

I first laid eyes on you I recognized you without the slightest hesitation. And from what borders did you come, so fearfully protected against everyone, what initiation to which no one or almost no one was admitted has consecrated what you are. When I saw you, all that fog, that unspeakable fog, was still in your eyes. How can one be born again, and above all *who* can one be born again after the loss of a being, a child who is everything one cherishes, with even more reason when her death is accidental and when in this child, almost a young woman, were objectively embodied (and you're not the only one who has told me this) all the grace, all the gifts of the mind, all the eagerness to know and experience, which reflect back to life a bewitching image, always in motion, through a completely new game, insanely complicated and delicate, of sieves and prisms? I didn't know anything about this drama: I only saw you dressed in a blue shadow like the one reeds are bathed in at the break of dawn and I couldn't have suspected that you came from even farther away, that with the crumbling of those prospects, so dear to you, you would even have given up your own, you couldn't help wanting to create pure night inside yourself and you almost succeeded, and that just one breech was all it took to call you back against all hope. Each time you recall these atrocious events, in my love I have no other recourse but to keep watch in secret deep in your eyes over the signal that made that terrible railroad crossing do an abrupt about-face, while you were already so far away. It alone guarantees your omnipresence around me and the gradual receding, absolutely necessary, of zones whose contemplation at short range only reopens Medusa's eyelids. It alone has mastered everything appealing about the shadows. The halt to which it brought you was irrevocable and without appeal—whether you wanted it or not, you had been *let off*.

Since life wanted you against your will, you're not the kind who can only give it half of yourself. Even the pain and the dream of actually succumbing to it have only been doors for you, open to the always self-renewing need to bend, to sensitize, to embellish this cruel life. You know how I see it in you, nightingale feathers in its pageboy haircut. Its quivering has a hold on you, I know of nothing more touching than the idea that it completely recaptured you. The offense was so serious that only an equally powerful pardon could match it. *More beautiful*, the solution to this most dangerous enigma was to be more beautiful than you'd ever been. More beautiful for having pushed aside the Dominions of Angels. More beautiful for still knowing how to accept the day hour by hour, the grass blade by blade. More beautiful for taking a love potion again and for being well-bred enough to have brought it to your lips without reservation, disregarding what terrible bitterness it may have contained. It required nothing less than all the forces that appear in fairy tales to make the fragrant flower emerge from the cinders, to make the white beast leap, its long eye unveiling the mystery of the woods.

Pipe organs of human love; by the sea, with its completely abstract motion engulfed by the city; opening under the midnight sun, even in a hovel, the sinuous windows of ice castles; in dizzy spells that smooth their wings preparing to sideswipe, now the whole sweep of a spring evening, now the echo endlessly ambushed in a verse or in some phrase in a book, now the moaning of that copper star weighing several tons, which a vow of a peculiar nature has suspended from a chain uniting two peaks hundreds of yards above a village of the Lower-Alps: Moustiers-Sainte-Marie. That love—nothing will prevent me from persisting in seeing it as the true panacea, no matter how embattled it may be, decried and mocked for religious and other reasons. Putting aside all fallacious ideas incapable of redemption, it's precisely by love and by love alone that the fusion of existence and essence is realized in the highest sense, it alone succeeds in immediately reconciling, completely harmoniously and unequivocally, these two notions, while without it they remain forever nervous and hostile. Naturally I am speaking of the love that *seizes power,* that allows itself a whole lifetime, that of course only consents to find its object in one single being. In this regard, experience, even if adverse, has taught me nothing. As far as I'm concerned, this possibility is still just as strong as ever and I know I could renounce it only at the expense of sacrificing everything I live by. A very powerful myth continues to have a hold on me, and no apparent contradiction of it in the course of my previous adventures can prevail. "Find the place and the formula" merges with, "possess truth in one soul and one body;" that highest hope has the power to unfold before it the allegorical arena which holds that every human being was thrown into life to search for a being of the opposite sex and only that one who is paired in all respects, to the point where one without the other seems like the result of the dissociation, of the dismembering of a unit of light. Happiest are those who succeed in reassembling this unit. Attraction by itself cannot be a reliable guide. Love, even the kind I'm speaking of, must, alas, also be able to play the game. In the jungle of solitude, a beautiful flick of a fan can be mistaken for paradise. But to be the first to denounce love is to acknowledge that one has not begun with the loftiest premise. No difficulties can arise in sustaining it: the unit once rejoined thwarts any divisiveness by its very structure; it's characterized by the property that between the component parts there exists a foolproof physical and mental bond.

Such an idea, if it still appears daring, presides more or less explicitly over the letters of Eloise, over the plays of Shakespeare and Ford, over the letters of the Portuguese Nun, over all of Novalis' works, it illuminates Thomas Hardy's beautiful book, *Jude the Obscure*. In the most general sense, love only thrives on requital, from which it doesn't at all follow that it is necessarily requited, a much lesser sentiment being capable of casually taking pleasure in admiring itself in it, indeed in exulting in it for a while. But requited love is the only one which conditions us for a total magnetization, which nothing can have a hold on, which makes flesh into sun and a resplendent imprint on the flesh, which turns the mind into an eternally welling spring, unalterable and always lively, whose water heads once and for all between the forget-me-nots and the wild thyme.

It will be a beautiful day, I see it filtering through your eyes where it began, cloudier, by being so beautiful. They come from that very water, from the points where it glides in the sunlight over the blue flints and the arch which hangs high over them comes from the finest, most sensitive gleam of the marten, not from the reflections it can delight, but the quivering of this gleam distracted only by the thought of the coat of this graceful, wary animal. Some gunshots are flaking off again in the distance! And, by lightning, the oblique image of the trap, with its contrary and doubly inexorable will, is enlarged totally out of proportion in the grass. Like the apple of her eye, it's this familiar expression which takes account of what we value above all else: so there came a day when you could no longer cherish the apple of your eyes, your eyes which fate wanted me to come into later on to make the sunlight well up in them. What magic ribbon is unravelling here. Life, like freedom, only comes to know itself when it has been struck, when it has been partially ravished; only then does it rise to total awareness of its means and resources, does it radiate with full brilliance in the eyes of another. At every moment its triumph is stunning and candid like the flowers which, once winter is over, spring from the rubble. In your eyes is the first dew of those flowers and your lips have an affinity for words in always freshly iridescent necklaces that make whirlpools lavish. And you are also beautiful with the beauty which has always captivated men, with the beauty that they dread and honor in the person of Helen, with the beauty which even fate pursues in vain, whose eternal justification for others and for itself, if it is necessary, is contained in these mysterious words: "I am Helen." And that beauty, for those who can recognize it, seems to have a certain claim on you, in that you were not as free to disappear as you were to reappear with the mask of pain or weariness, that you continued to have to answer to life with all the fire of your heart. It's possible that beauty only gives itself completely at that price. A touch, the most sumptuous one of all, will always be missing if circumstances spare it from being so tempered by fire. The mountaintop takes on a divine form only in the mist of your glance, only in the golden eagle's wing passing over your hair. And I love you because the sea air and the mountain air, mixed here in their original purity, are no more exempt from miasmas and no more intoxicating than the air of your soul where the largest squall has already come and gone, solemnly and strictly confirming it in its natural propensity to resolve everything, starting with life's minutest difficulties, by an outpouring of your boundless generosity which would in itself be sufficient evidence for what is distinctly your own: the absolute sense of *grandeur*.

Here, under your light step, is a parapet of such dubious stability that it has to be propped up at night with heavy stones, but no matter how firm it seems, nothing prevents the storm from treating it like a straw plaything, here is the fine sand studded with umbels by the birds' feet. From a few miles away, Bonaventure Island continues to loom: legend has it that it was the den of an ogre who, crossing this body of water in one stride, came to grab the women and maids of the coast, with whom he filled his vast pockets. Once back home with his meal finished, he washed his clothes in the high tide and lay them out to dry on the tall cliffs. There could be no better way for the folk imagination to account for the incriminating and radiant persistence of the maculation of the rock, the superhuman efforts and the prodigious quantity of perpetually gushing soapy lather formed by the white plumage which was powerless to make it disappear. What detergent, no less strong, will succeed in wiping from the human spirit the great collective scars and the throbbing memories of these days of hatred! What sacred refuge will they have to build in their hearts for all ideas which, like the gannets on their nests, will struggle to put an end to this period or, with their sumptuous and free flight, will combine to transform the face of this tragic battlement! What choice place will be reserved for feelings of love, like the niches on the flanks of the rock, key to the whole display, where we were shown birds taking shelter two by two! Love, poetry, art, it's only through their resilience that confidence will return, that human thought will succeed in setting sail again. We will not be able to count on science again until it forms its own clear picture of how to remedy the strange curse that has fallen on it and which seems to doom it to accumulate so many more mistakes and calamities than benefits. Without prejudice to the measures of moral disinfection which are being imposed on this somber eve of twice the year one thousand and which are essentially social acts, for a man considered by himself there can be no more valuable and far-reaching hope than in the beat of a wing.

Here again, perpendicular to the wave crests, to that barely sinuous stippled water line that the agate hunters return to each day in single file, is Percé Rock itself, as it is cut by our window frames and as I'll take its image with me when I'm long gone from here. Working my way around it a little earlier I regretted not being able, from so close up, to discover its totality, and that new arrangements of its mass gave rise to images different from those I had already formed. One can only retain the last image when it's a question of picturing such complex structures. Besides, it's above all from that angle, that is, seen from the west, that it has caught the eye of photographers. "Percé Rock: 280 feet from the top to the prow, 250 feet at its widest point, 1,420 feet long," a tourist brochure says laconically and if I don't mind copying these figures it's because I wouldn't be surprised if in the relationship of these dimensions the *golden section* should appear, Percé Rock being in its proportions that good a model of natural precision. It presents two parts to us which, from where I'm accustomed to observe them, seem to lead a separate existence, the first initially suggesting a vessel on which an ancient musical instrument has been superimposed, the second a head with its profile missing a little something, a head with a haughty bearing, with a heavy Louis XIV wig. As the prow of the ship drives its north end towards the beach, a wide opening greets us at its base, at the level of the rear mast. Rising above the sea to a height of sixty feet or so, that opening could, only a few years ago, before some cave-ins created an obstacle, serve as a passage for sailboats. It will always remain essential to the emotional appreciation of the monument, and in it lies its truly unique quality. No matter what its diminutiveness relative to the hull it undermines, in effect the opening gives access to the idea that the imagined boat is also an *ark* and it is admirable that the currents which break all along the wall find there an outlet where they are even more frenetically swallowed up. This breach alone is undoubtedly what dictates the secondary resemblance to a sort of distant pipe organ, more this instrument than any other since the day when, searching to identify the face and the posture of the stone head turned towards it, you thought it might be the head of Handel, quickly correcting yourself with: Handel? no, definitely Bach.

Geologists and paleontologists reach new peaks of pleasure all over the Gaspé peninsula where they calculate the immemorial landslides, of which a pebble dressed as a harlequin, uniformly polished by the sea, sometimes gives solitary testimony. Superb fragments, passed from hand to hand, are found in the area of Grand Grève, fragments on which winged towers of trilobites crisscross in every direction, suggesting the most heavily worked tablets of Benin even while dissociating themselves as far as possible with the play of their beige, silver, and lilac lights. In everything one treads on, there is something that comes from so much farther back than mankind and which is also going so much farther. Naturally, this is true anywhere, but is more palpable in a place where every footstep brings a properly detailed reminder. A perspective results from this, far different from the one which, in the short run, has a tendency to prevail in cities. The great enemy of mankind is opacity. This opacity is outside him and above all within him, where conventional ideas and all sorts of dubious defenses maintain it. Sometimes one catches oneself thinking that the fate of the human race was played out forever in a series of events quite far from being completely random, but which an invincible laziness has confirmed as established fact, and which we have scruples about reversing. Yet it seems that the game could have been played very differently and above all that the ever more universal calamities that mark its development should attest to the fact that in many respects it has begun very poorly. At the top of the list of initial errors that remain the most detrimental stands the idea that the universe only has intelligible meaning for mankind, and that it has none, for instance, for animals. Man prides himself on being the chosen one of creation. Everything that evolution has been able to reveal to him about his origins and general biological necessities, which even assign a limit to the duration of his species, remains in effect a dead letter. He persists in seeing and acting as though these revelations, so crushing to his pride, never occurred. Even the reservations which philosophers have taught him to have about his capacity for understanding never enter into his plans except for the sake of appearances and in his heart of hearts do not dissuade him in the least from treating all final causes as if they necessarily refer to him. Incessant disappointments have never succeeded in making him aware of the indigence of his criteria. The gift of gab that has fallen to his lot and the baffling optimism which he is endowed with lead him boisterously to congratulate himself on the state of his knowledge, even though most people live with a real and increasing lack of curiosity, and even though his knowledge, more and more centered around immediate comforts (which are only a mockery of progress), never misses a chance to turn thunderously against him. His ideas are a *summary*, yes a summary of postulates without rigor, which could have been different and continue imperturbably to spin out their consequences even though a good number of them have been definitively invalidated. No matter what happens, the fate of these ideas appears to be that they are no longer capable of climbing back up the path they once took. From birth man finds them in narrow channels and he is only free to push them forward along a road that has already been laid out. This road is lined with buildings—the church, school, the barracks, the factory, the bar, the bank, again the church—and statues, among them the solid ones, truly rare, bearing witness to real glories, can very gradually be distinguished from the hollow ones, innumerable, which tend to commemorate usurped glory. (The latter, what's more, are not proving to be the less unshakeable ones—let it suffice to cite the example of La Fontaine, called with antiphrasis, "good old La Fontaine," and despite the protestations before my own of Jean-Jacques Rousseau and Jean-Henri Fabre, La Fontaine continues, with no claim whatsoever to pass for a poet, to enjoy in France the stupefying prerogative of being the first instructor of our young.) Yet one searches in vain among this throng of pedestals and steles for the great adventurers of the mind, for those who grabbed man by the arm, who summoned him to know himself in depth or who called on him to justify his so-called ideas—their names are Paracelsus, Rousseau, Sade, Lautréamont, Freud, their names are Marat, Saint-Just ... on this side the list would be long. And yet those I'm citing, with barely one or two exceptions, never committed a revolutionary act except in relative terms. How long will we have to wait for a brand new laboratory where established ideas, *no matter which,* beginning with the most elementary ones, the ones most hastily exonerated, will be accepted only for purposes of study, contingent on an examination *from top to bottom* and by definition free from all preconceptions? I say that one day these ideas should no longer lay claim to being accepted, they should only be taken note of for the sake of inventory. In particular, it seems to me that it will be impossible to appear *a priori* too severe in approaching logic, which has contributed its full, withering measure to our time, and that morality can not pretend without being impudent to do more than conciliate the greatest number of human interests, which requires from the outset that it renounce founding itself on superlunary considerations or on the worthless residues of them. It is essential, it is urgent that we remedy the limiting and distressing aspects of the concept of *time*, at least as it has been developed in the West and, correlatively, to obviate (from one point of view this is even more compellingly necessary) the way so-called civilized man continues to make death into a bogeyman, while on this point the savage is, by comparison, a model of dignity. It's at this price and only at this price that the great cries of humanity which have always been suppressed, the desire for truth, for beauty, dare I say for goodness, and in any case the power of love, could succeed in gaining the upper hand and in regenerating the world as quickly as it has been destroyed. Then vast fields of discovery could open up next to which those we know would be meager lots horribly fenced in. We want, said Apollinaire, oddly enough in his last poem,

> *"We want to explore goodness, enormous*
> *land where all is silent."*

Yielding to the pressure of centuries, his only mistake in this poem was to apologize for it.

To begin with, we should put an end to the idea that human culture, as disseminated by textbooks, is the product of an orderly and predetermined activity, when it is constructed on the arbitrary and had to agree to follow the general route that routine accorded it. There is absolutely nothing inevitable about the fact that it has reached this or that level, because nothing in its very essence conflicted with its developing, if not freely, then at least under very different constraints. No determinism, valid within its own framework, justifies the aplomb of the majority of ideas that are transmitted from one era to another and onto which are grafted along the way a minimum of original ideas that refrain from transgressing against the earlier ones except in regard to certain details. Today's education is entirely defective to the extent that, calling itself positivist, it begins with abusing the child's trust by presenting as true what is only either a temporary phenomenon, or a hypothesis, when it's not a blatant untruth; and to the extent that it prevents children from forming in good time their own opinions by creasing into them certain habits that make their freedom of judgment an illusion. Even facts presented as true to life, which their memories become encumbered with, and which are served as food for their young rapture, are exaggerated or minimized, or indeed mixed in with fictions, or at the very least put forward in a tendentious manner in the service of a cause of which the least one can say is that it is not that of humanity but in reality of a certain caste of individuals. For example, one has only to flip through an elementary French history textbook—and I'm not even speaking of the revised and expurgated editions that may have been distributed over the last few years—to surprise in *flagrant délit* those with the audacity to pull on gloves to operate on virgin minds and usually only succeed in maiming them forever. Down with Robespierre, besides, Louis x v i was a good king, though a little on the weak side *(sic)*, but the true national hero will continue to be honored in the person of Napoleon: those are the generally indelible ideas which the French Republic allows to be inculcated in children of whom the majority will not go beyond an elementary school education. We're lucky that the very conscious class of teachers took every possible liberty with this curriculum. Nevertheless, it's not that scandalous bias, that incorrigibly reactionary spirit which most struck me in this matter, but all those who contrive to match the above mentioned historians with mythographers, with only this difference—all to their detriment—that the former claim as exact what the latter expose as mythic. Above all it is when we stop to think of the illustrations in those scholarly books— illustrations the memory of which, I maintain, will haunt generations, that one can't defend such a confusion. These illustrations, in fact, do not aid in understanding the text, nor do they comment on the most salient episodes and this observation could also be made of the anecdotes called upon to impress young minds and which are apt to take a bizarrely unnecessary turn, in any case irrational and at the same time very concrete: their thread seems to unreel completely on the margins of historical relations in the proper sense and I can't help, from a distance, seeing in them a very marked occult character. Their pattern is to a great extent different from that of the general picture which it no longer fits except in certain outlines. What's more, it seems that secret symbolic intentions creep in here: old men dressed in white harvest the mistletoe from the oak trees using golden sickles, "Remember the vase of Soissons," Charlemagne visits a school and scolds the rich children, Phillip the Fair mints counterfeit coins, Charles VI has an upsetting encounter in Le Mans Forest, a young shepherdess kneeling is instructed by Saint Michael and Saint Catherine, the latter at the stake, Henry III and his "pets" playing with the cup-and-ball, Henry IV making a certain Mayenne lose its breath along a coastline, the Gray Eminence, the Sun King, the young Louis x v kills the birds in an aviary, that excellent Louis x v i devotes his leisure time to the locksmith's trade (and as for the French Revolution, the pupil is gently advised that he'll hear about it when he's older), the many facets of Napoleon, his hat, etc., but of the nineteenth century just enough so that the book can close with a pretty view of the Place de l'Opéra. Can one imagine a more perfect disdain for true proportion and couldn't one say that the author is following a much less naive design than his mild-mannered language would lead one to believe, and that he is less concerned with testifying truthfully than with acting on the unconscious by using a parable whose meaning and unity he grasps and which puts at his mercy those who are only urged to learn it *literally?* This ambiguous behavior alone, in a domain where the most rigorous authenticity must be the rule, should always evoke the deepest suspicions. Among established ideas, ideas about history, as long as history is written in a national framework, should elicit our strongest reservations. Here as elsewhere, but particularly here, a prolonged bath of skepticism is advisable with all due dispatch. There can be no question of a new humanism until the day when history, rewritten after discussion by all peoples and *limited to just one version*, will agree to make its subject *all* of mankind, as far as documentation permits, and to take account completely objectively of past deeds and gestures without any special regard for the land where so and so lives and for the language he speaks. Art and science, in their own fields, come close to experiencing this state of grace: it's hard to see why this couldn't be extended to the other branches of intellectual activity. Is it necessary to state that we see nothing dawning to announce this truce among all these unreasonable passions, a truce out of which less cruel times could emerge.

Dear shadows trapped for so long in a crossfire, yesterday almost beaten back, Charles Fourier's frenetic shadow, Flora Tristan's shadow forever rustling, Father Enfantin's delicious shadow, the jeers meted out to you will not be right forever, and let me add that they alone should be enough to predispose poets in your favor. You're owed major reparations, current events lay the groundwork for them, these events may even bring them quite close and the reparations will be all the more dazzling for being so late. In vain sociology has put on airs, proclaiming a bit too insistently that it has reached adulthood, I don't see why it should have the right to slap with ridicule and charges of inconsistency contributions like yours where a daring that so far knows no bounds has never ceased putting itself in the service of the greatest generosity. The jibes which, in art, accumulated, without succeeding in discouraging him, around the efforts of the customs inspector Rousseau, dedicated to developing his potential for instinctive expression outside the precepts of academia, the indifference of some vaguely condescending people who continue to take target practice on the postman Cheval, who succeeded, despite the worst of circumstances, in giving form to his dream, are reflecting back today or will reflect back tomorrow on those who thought they could be great wits at their expense. For me the thing that was always passionately compelling about works like theirs was that they dropped a bombshell on their era, that they were created completely outside the cultural line of an era, and also that they pay much greater tribute than others to the aspirations and fears which form the common ground of humanity. If the demands of humanity are to have a chance to partially triumph in the practical sphere, they must take pains with specifics, and for this reason get science in their camp; then the only thing left is, at the risk of an emotional impoverishment which would make them sterile and, to tell the truth, already threatens them, they must retemper and recast themselves in the *unbridled* desire for improvement of the collective condition, very quickly denounced as utopian by those who individually take umbrage at it. Might I add with all due respect to the great and hardly indulgent figures who preside over the destiny of scientific socialism, and whose distant, disdainful expression has already been wrenched from them by those who cite them as authorities; great brandies can't make us pity unclouded wines. For their excesses and for all that originates in their imaginative intoxication, one can't help but concede to the reformist writers of the first half of the nineteenth century, exactly as with primitive artists, the beneficial effect of extreme freshness. That freshness is what we're particularly thirsting for today. On the social plane as elsewhere, we may hope that out of the unprecedented ideological confusion that will mark the end of this war will arise a fairly large number of radical propositions formulated *outside the existing framework* and which, braving accusations of ingenuousness and of gratuitous and inconsequential conjecture, and faced with the temporary bankruptcy of the language of the mind, will make the language of the heart and the senses heard loud and clear. We fully expect this language to restore to their places of honor the great themes which are unique to it—that the flesh is as sacred as the soul, that they can not be sundered—and may we be ruled by the idea of *the salvation of the earth by woman*, of the transcendent vocation of woman, a vocation which has been systematically concealed, thwarted, or led astray to our day, but which nevertheless will be triumphantly affirmed one day, according to the supreme claim of Goethe himself.

To describe the geometry of an era that has not yet come full circle requires an appeal to an ideal observer, removed from the contingencies of that era, which implies from the start the need for an ideal observation post and, if everything prevents me from placing myself in the role of this observer, it seems to me equally true that no place fulfills the necessary requirements as well as Percé Rock, as it unfolds to me at certain times of day. It's when, at nightfall or on certain foggy mornings, the details of its structure become cloudy that the image of a sloop, always imperiously commanded, can be refined from it. Aboard, everything points to the infallible glance of the captain, but a captain who would also be a magician. It's as if the vessel, just a short while ago bereft of riggings, seems suddenly to be equipped for the most vertiginous of ocean voyages. In fact it is said that the water which accumulates in autumn in the crevices of the rock freezes there in winter, repeatedly causing the crust to overstretch, producing annually about three hundred tons of scree. The experts in this field have not, of course, spared us the childish arithmetical calculation, which once we've reckoned the total weight of the rock at four million tons, allows us to deduce the aggregate time it will take to disappear, that is, thirteen thousand years. However unwarranted this calculation may be, at least it has the virtue of setting the enormous vessel in motion, of providing it with motors whose power is comparable to the very slow and yet very noticeable process of disintegration that it's undergoing. It's beautiful, it's moving that its longevity is not limitless and at the same time that it covers such a succession of human lives. In its depths there is more than enough time to see born and die a city like Paris where gun shots are reverberating right now even inside Notre Dame as the great rose window turns. And now that great rose window whirls and twirls in the rock: without a doubt these shots were the prearranged signal because *the curtain is rising.* It has been claimed that, faced with Percé Rock, the pen and the brush must admit their impotence and it's true that those who are called upon to speak least superficially about it will think they have said it all when they have attested to the magnificence of this curtain, when their voices suddenly deepened to depict its dark radiance, when they have succeeded in creating some order out of the modulation of the mass of air that vibrates in its majestically discordant pipes. But, lacking the knowledge that it's a curtain, how could they suspect that its staggering drapery hides a set with many levels? And to begin with, behind it arises, in the way of a prologue, a children's story which only serves to adjust the lighting: the tough one with the frozen white hair can hardly see any more; she no longer knows how to make her witch's recipe for bringing down the house, except in the large pots by the front door. No matter how angry she is that she can't smash everything to smithereens, every time she goes out she has to remember to turn the key twice to lock in the little girl who cares for her snowy owl. But the bird won the child's trust by telling her about the northern lights: in exchange for its freedom, it taught her the secret of how to instantaneously light up, in whatever corner she wished of the bitter room, an eye, sparkling and intent as her own—all she needed to do was to touch an empty hazel nut shell with a moist straw from the broom. Since this game proves to be extremely engrossing and since the little girl, by listening to the owl, acquired eyesight so penetrating she could throw a party in the eye of a needle, she soon ran the magic straw through every possible orifice, from the little holes in the ladle to the keyhole, from the eyelet of an old shoe to every last buttonhole. And these all began not only to see, but to radiate light, and all the lights began to connect while keeping the distinctive qualities of their sources: some came out of a blue almond framing a window behind which a lamp was lit, others came from a large hailstone beginning to melt on a dusty street, others from a skein of faded green silk under the claw of a black cat, others from blood drying on the finger of a beautiful Arab woman, pricked on a rosebush. Wherever I insert this little girl—I'd like her to be jumping rope inside stones—in order to depict even a single agate from Percé, chemists will insist on seeing only silica which, carried by water, is deposited and crystallized in mineral cavities. But the little girl only had to head for the broom to send them running. It's done: all the lights have connected. The old ramshackle cottage doesn't exist any more, the broom has been turned into an egret that struts the whole length of the rock. The egret's body has quite naturally placed itself in the opening of the breach, right where I absolutely loved positioning myself so as to see the sunrise through it, and it's this misty body that supports all of the now weightless arch. On a revolving stage, a chain of white elephants fold their legs in rhythm with the wind and the seas in order to make the moons in their toenails turn with the beat, brandishing their trunks at the sky, generating with their imperceptible sway alone the now *transparent* image of the rock. Where just a while ago one could only see serpentine bands of quartz, the trunks in their turn are lost in the diffused light, giving way to a thousand heralds carrying streamers who scatter in all directions. In these bright ship flags fringed with gold, no one would think of recognizing all the coarse material that was hoisted and is still being hoisted above the risky undertakings of mankind. And yet it's the great swell of those banners, dominated, as we've seen, by the rejection of the jolly roger and subject to a dazzling transmutation, which takes hold of the rock to the point of seeming to make up its whole substance. And the proclamation, trumpeted to the four winds, actually is important since the shouts of beaming mouths trimmed with shot silk echo in every direction only the eternal newsflash: the terrible curse has been lifted, all power for the regeneration of the world lies in human love. "And a strong angel picked up a rock like a large grindstone and flung it into the sea, saying, 'With such clatter and vehemence shall fall this great Babylon and it shall be heard of no more.'" But the prophecy fails to mention that there's another rock like a large grindstone that is its exact counterweight on the scale of the waves, that it's rising tumultuously, ardently, even faster than the other is sinking: it's the love of man and woman which lies, hypocrisy, and psychological misery still hold back from showing what it's capable of, which to be born has historically had to foil the vigilance of the furious old religions, and which only began to stammer so late, in the songs of the troubadours. And in the rising stone, still *one* with the rock that I contemplate, are braced, pierced with all the rays of the moon, the buttresses of old chateaus of Aquitaine and elsewhere in the background the Chateau of Montségur, still burning. That window caught there in the ivy, that window with red stained glass striated with lightning, is Juliet's window. That room, on the second floor of an out-of-the-way valley inn, where a door left open lets in all the musicians of the stream, is the one where Kleist, ready to disarm solitude forever, spent his final night. That pale tower, along which is spreading a blond waterfall which comes to disappear into the sand, that tower is Mélisande's, as if her eyes, collecting a downpour of April swallows, and her trees-in-bloom mouth were near me in this cabin we're looking out of. In the rising stone, now totally clouded over with blue but scratched with roving vermilion flashes—as though brave blood can never fail—one can still see the vessel raising anchor, its smokestacks vomiting in great scrolls the defeated hypnotist *who is not at all the one they said,* but actually the boa constrictor who was coiled in the path of the heavy, meandering boulder and who, when Thought left here for other regions, came to hiss, not to mention open its triangular mouth in the crack. That's him, there was time enough to recognize him, the maker of both opacity and unhappiness, the one who wins without a fight: "Neither dead nor living. Fog. Mud. Shapeless," he who identifies himself to the young Peer Gynt as: *The Big Curve.* No doubt he will be reborn, more impudent and cowardly than ever, from the false repentances and from the laughable impulses for improvement that will be paid out in pennyroyal at the end of this war. Yet that ark remains, and even if I can't make everyone see it, it's filled with all the fragility but also with all the magnificence of human genius. Set in its marvelous moonstone iceberg, it's driven by three glass helices which are love, but as it arises invulnerably between two beings; art, but art arrived at its highest point; and the all-out struggle for freedom. Observed more absentmindedly from the shore, Percé Rock only has wings because of its birds.

MELUSINA AFTER THE SCREAM, Melusina be low the bust, I see her scales mirrored in the autumn sky. Her radiant coil twists three times around a wooded hill, which undulates in waves that follow a score where all the harmonies are tuned to, and reverberate with, those of the nasturtium in bloom. Logging has opened its slopes to skiing, at least that's all profane interpretation confines itself to, but then one must admit that well before the snowfall their curves are glazed with the most beautiful frost, blue frost which, when one takes care to avoid in wandering all beaten or even faint trails—and that should be the only rule in art—comes along to interject, all in diamonds, its despairing palm branches on the painter's imaginary windows. Melusina, it's really her marvelous, dramatic tail disappearing between the fir trees in the little lake taking on over there the taper and color of a saber. Yes, it's always the lost woman, the one who sings in man's imagination but at the end of such trials for her, for him, that it must also be the woman who's found again. And first woman must find herself, must, without man's more than problematical help, learn to recognize herself through the hells to which she is doomed by the view that man, in general, has of her. So many times, in the course of this war and before that in the preceding one, I waited to hear that scream ring out, the scream buried for nine centuries under the ruins of the Chateau of Lusignan! Woman is, after all, the great victim of these military endeavors. I will never forget the arms of womankind, on certain nights in Paris at the Gare de l'Est, the admirable, the staggering image they formed. It was less her face than her arms which, in the *already rarified and false* air, had assumed that unique quality. The arms of women who really loved, who lost everything, that arm of Ingres' Thetis, that arm made to hold back and to halt, and that arm whose laxity in the articulation of the elbow renders a mere nothing so moving and disquieting, that permits it to bend back a little (under these circumstances the possibility of such a gesture becomes tragic). All of womanhood, all that has not been irremediably separated from the way of feeling that is hers alone, enters the luxurious, prodigious movement of that arm, a movement, as I just recounted, given such a strange limit that it risks dislocating itself if it rises in rebellion. And all of that has been defied, humiliated, and denied as much as possible by the workings of a war, the physical instigation of which no woman worthy of the name participates in, unless her life or those of her loved ones are directly threatened. I've always been stupefied that she didn't make her voice heard, that she didn't think of taking every possible advantage, the immense advantage of the two irresistible and priceless inflections given to her, one for talking to men during love, the other that commands all of a child's trust. What clout, what future would this great cry of warning and refusal from woman have had, this always powerful cry whose potential, because of a dreamlike evil spell, so many beings do not succeed in realizing, if in the course of the last few years it could have sprung up, especially in Germany, and if impossibly it might have been strong enough to resist being stifled! After so many female "saints" and national heroines fanning the combativeness of this or that camp, when will we see a woman simply as woman perform quite a different *miracle* of extending her arms between those who are about to grapple to say: you are brothers. Is it because the yoke is crushing womankind that she doesn't see in such a case an opportunity to play her role, that she definitively abdicates before forces that are obviously opposed to her! This crisis is so severe that I, myself, see only one solution: the time has come to value the ideas of woman at the expense of those of man, whose bankruptcy is coming to pass fairly tumultuously today. It is artists, in particular, who must take the responsibility, if only to protest against this scandalous state of affairs, to maximize the importance of everything that stands out in the feminine world view in contrast to the masculine, to build only on woman's resources, to exalt, or even better to appropriate to the point of jealously making it one's own, all that distinguishes her from man in terms of modes of appreciation and volition. If the truth were told, this direction I'd like art to take is not new: for quite some time art has implicitly complied with it in great measure and the later we move into the modern period, the more we can say that this predilection has become pronounced, that it tends to monopolize. Rémy de Gourmont will be paid back for his insult to Rimbaud: "A girl's temperament," said he. Today, a judgment of this sort shows us the measure of the one who made it: it tells us all we need to build a case against the male type of intelligence at the end of the nineteenth century. On the one hand the great sweep of a wing, nothing less than "change life," on the other the slobber of a book-eating rat. Let's just look at what time has done to these two attitudes: we see the mind, on one side in a gradual and ever more sure ascent, on the other constantly losing energy. Justice has already been done, I only ask that in the future it be even more expeditious. Let art resolutely yield the passing lane to the supposedly "irrational" feminine, let it fiercely make enemies of all that which, having the effrontery to present itself as sure and solid, bears in reality the mark of that masculine intransigence which, in the field of human relations at the international level, shows well enough today what it is capable of. I say that the time is past when we can be satisfied on this point by mere whims, by more or less shameful concessions; instead, those of us in the arts must pronounce ourselves unequivocally against man and for woman, bring man down from a position of power which, it has been sufficiently demonstrated, he has misused, restore this power to the hands of woman, dismiss all of man's pleas so long as woman has not yet succeeded in taking back her fair share of that power, not only in art but in life.

Melusina after the scream... The lake sparkles, it's a ring and yet it's the whole sea passing through the Doge's wedding band, because the whole living universe must bless this alliance and nothing more can sunder it. Melusina below the bust is gilded by all the reflections of the sun off the fall foliage. The snakes of her legs dance to the beat of the tambourine, the fish of her legs dive and their heads reappear elsewhere as if hanging from the words of that saint who preached among the scorpion grass, the birds of her legs drape her with airy netting. Melusina half-reclaimed by panic-stricken life,

Melusina with lower joints of broken stones or aquatic plants or the down of a nest, she's the one I invoke, she's the only one I can see who could redeem this savage epoch. She's all of woman and yet woman as she exists today, woman deprived of her human base, prisoner of her mobile roots, if you will, but also through them in providential communication with nature's elemental forces. Woman deprived of her human base, legend has it, by the impatience and jealousy of man. Only a long meditation by man on his error, a long penitence proportionate to the suffering that resulted from it, can restore that base to her. Because Melusina, before and after her metamorphosis, *is* Melusina.

Melusina no longer under the burden of the fate unleashed on her by man alone, Melusina rescued, Melusina before the scream that will announce her return, because that scream could not have been heard if it hadn't been reversible, like the stone of the Apocalypse and like all things. Melusina's first scream was a bouquet of ferns beginning to writhe in a tall chimney, it was the most frail Chinese junk breaking from its moorings at night, it was the white-hot blade of a lightning bolt right in front of the eyes of all the birds in the woods. Melusina's second scream will definitely be the dip of a child's swing in a garden where there is no swing, it will definitely be young caribou frolicking in a glade, it will definitely be the dream of childbirth without pain.

Melusina at the instant of her second scream: she sprang up off her globeless haunches, her belly is the whole August harvest, her torso bursts into fireworks from her arched back, modelled on a swallow's two wings, her breasts are two ermines caught in their own scream, blinding because they are lit by scorching coals of their howling mouth. And her arms are the soul of streams that sing and float perfumes. And under the landslide of her tarnished hair all the distinctive traits of the child-woman take shape, that distinctive type that has always conquered poets *because time on her has no hold.*

The child-woman. Systematically art must prepare her advent into the empire of tangible things. It must constantly keep her in mind in its triumphs, making the bats turn tail with their sickening syllogistic flight while the glowworms spin at its command the mysterious thread which alone leads to the heart of the labyrinth. This creature exists and, if she is not endowed with complete awareness of her power, it is nevertheless true that she's the apparition you see from farther and farther away at the railroad switch, briefly commanding the delicate cogs of the nervous system. And she's Bilqis with eyes so long that even in profile they seem full face, and she's Cleopatra on the morning of Actium, and she's the young sorceress of Michelet with the eyes of a heath, and she's Bettina by the side of a waterfall speaking for her brother and her fiancé, and she is—even more devious because of her very impassiveness—Gustave Moreau's fairy with the griffon, and she's you. What stores of felinity, of daydreams that can conquer life, of inward fire strong enough to face the flames, of mischief in the service of genius and, above all, of strange calm permeated with the glow of a watchman's lantern, are contained in those instants when beauty, as if to extend the range of visibility, suddenly makes it all in vain, lets the vain restlessness of man die for her. These explosive moments are charged with such force! The figure of the child-woman sends fissures through the best organized systems because nothing has been able to subdue or encompass her. Her temperament disarms all severity beginning with, I can't tell her too many times, that of the years. Even the blows which fall on her strengthen her, make her more supple, refine her still more and when all is said and done, complete her like the chisel of an ideal sculptor, obeying the laws of a pre-established harmony which is never realized because, when false steps are not possible, he is on the road to perfection and that road can never end. And even the body's death, the physical destruction of a work is not, in this case, an end. The radiance subsists, how should I put this, it's the whole statue, even more beautiful, if that's possible, which, in waking into the imperishable without losing any of its carnal appearance, derives its substance from a sublime intersection of rays.

Who will give the living scepter back to the child-woman? Who will discover the method in her reactions, still unknown even to her, in her wishes so hastily draped with the veil of capriciousness? For a long time he'll have to study her as she looks in the mirror and to begin with, he'll have to reject all the types of reasoning which men are so shabbily proud of, which they're so miserably duped by, make a clean slate of the principles which man's psychology has so egotistically been built on, *which have absolutely no validity for woman,* in order to advise women's psychology in its trials with its predecessor, with the ultimate responsibility of reconciling them. I choose the child-woman not in order to oppose her to other women, but because it seems to me that in her and in her alone exists in a state of absolute transparency the *other* prism of vision which they obstinately refuse to take into account, because it obeys very different laws whose disclosure male despotism must try to prevent at all costs.

From head to toe Melusina has become a woman again. With day having fallen a long time ago, and with novels of knighthood in the attic having regained their particularly cloying odor of dust, she has reclaimed the empty frame which even her image disappeared from in the middle of the feudal period. But little by little the wall inside the borders of the frame is hollowed out, fades away. The frame is none other than that of a window looking out on the darkness. That darkness is total, one might say it's that of our own time. Splendid Melusina, now that she's just been found again, one trembles with the fear that she'll entirely vanish in there. Nothing but the howling of wolves. The frame is hopelessly empty. Staring at it fixedly only gives rise to images of wraiths subject to the worst possible torments, the worst jealousies. These faces from a blind Bosch, without consistency or color, all with horrible expressions and undergoing the most awful transformations, stay in view for a few seconds before lugubriously sliding down left and right to give way to the more frightening ones that follow, because this is a mob scene! A bad, short movie of night: they are a long way from giving up the space. Why no streetlight on this narrow and slippery street? Ah yes, I forgot ... sirens, their infamous turnstyle. This must be one of the short breaks they take to convey the danger. In those semi-detached houses, women in robes still have to get the sleepy-eyed, scared children down the stairs. Do not move forward: of course, this is no longer life. The silence now the worst of it. I run my hand over my forehead. Deceitful night. The rear of a car zips away, a trapdoor or a pile of coal? Must be another *lecture* is about to begin and from a completely different window, I bet, it's the same show: a pile of coal, a trapdoor or a car zipping away? Some will concoct schemes with no vision while others will make much of or dissimulate sordid interests, because neither have understood: it is actually their common reference points which are wanting, which are false. So much for the future, as they believe they can manage it, at least... They haven't changed in twenty years and the very same ones are getting ready to start the whole thing over. Only with great difficulty can we interest ourselves in them and in fact they may not even hope for that: they are the gentlemen at the funeral.

I've closed my eyes to pray for the return of true night, night with its mask of terrors removed, night the supreme regulator and consolation, the great virgin night of *Hymns to the Night*. We had to wait for the confusion to clear from its surface, give it time to rest. Now it has taken up permanent residence in the frame that it fills to the breaking point with its myriad facets. It's bottomless as a diamond and only those lovers who have been able perilously to isolate themselves to lean over it from a window projecting above a park while in the distance the party rages on among crystal reeds and musical bubbles under the straps of the chandeliers, will know what mirrored vaults, what a lighthouse lens rose on such a night make a shining basket for their drunkenness, will be able to bear witness that it's only on such a night that the leaps of the heart and the senses find their infinite response.

All the magic of night is in the frame, all of night's enchantment. Perfumes and chills extravagate from the air into thoughts. The grace of life sends a muffled vibration through the flutes of Pan at the foot of the curtains. Besides, the black cube of the window is no longer so difficult to pierce: it is penetrated little by little by a brightness spread out in a garland, like a convolvulus of light attached to the two transversal edges at the top, not hanging below the upper third of the shape. The image gradually focuses into seven flowers which become stars while the lower part of the cube remains empty. The two highest stars are of blood, they represent the sun and moon; the five lower ones, alternating yellow and blue like sap, are the other planets known to the ancients. If the clock hadn't stopped at midnight, the little hand, without changing anything, could have gone four times around before a new glimmer emanated from the zenith which would dominate from above the first ones: a much brighter star is inscribed in the center of the original septenary and its points are of red and yellow fire and it's the Dog Star or Sirius, and it's Lucifer Light Bearer and it is, in its glory surpassing all the others, the Morning Star. The landscape doesn't light up till the very instant it appears, and at that instant life brightens again and immediately below the luminous blaze which just gave way to the ones just mentioned, a young woman is revealed, nude, kneeling by the side of a pond, and with her right hand she spills into the pond the contents of a golden urn, while her left hand empties onto the earth an equally inexhaustible silver urn. Alongside that woman who, beyond Melusina, is Eve and now is all womankind, the leaves of an acacia rustle to the right while to the left a butterfly flutters on a bloom.

When fate brought you to me, an enormous shadow was in me and I might even say it was inside me that the window opened. That revelation you brought me: before I even knew what it consisted of, I knew it was a revelation. I understood when I first laid eyes on you, when I heard your first words, that with a certain train of thought, despairing, vertiginous, and without brakes, when the machine of the mind goes so fast that it *jumps the tracks*, I must have touched one of the poles that generally remain out of reach, must have activated by chance that hidden little bell that summons *extraordinary rescues*. I have always believed in these rescues: it always seemed to me that an extreme tension in the manner of undergoing a moral test, not letting oneself be even imperceptibly distracted by it, not consenting one way or another to limit its ravages, by its very nature provoked such rescues and I believe, what's more, that I have verified this many a time. Whether it's a question of tests where everything leads you to believe that you will never pick yourself up again or lesser tests, I maintain that the correct action to take is to look them in the eye and to *let yourself flow*. I hold this to be true for pain as well as boredom. From an intellectual standpoint, it's when I've let myself get to the depths of my boredom that I've run into peculiar solutions, completely unsought at such moments, certain of which gave me reasons for living. But when you appeared, it was a completely different story. A large part of the globe was nothing more than a display of ruins. For myself, I had to really acknowledge, without resigning myself to it, that all that I had taken for indestructible in the realm of feeling had been swept away without my even knowing what gust did it: the only sign left was a child to whom, prey to the most justifiable fear, you may have heard me speak long ago. All the world's injustice and severity separated me from this child, deprived me of her beautiful awakenings which were my joy, made me lose with her contact with everyday marvels, and prepared to distance her from me even more. I wouldn't help in shaping her young mind which came to me so sparkling, so open. In me, too, there were ruins, forever blooming from that rose. And ideas, by which man tries to keep himself in a fixed relation to others, ideas weren't spared, either: more ruins, only facades remained standing, bulwarks of the Tower of

Babel. The words that delineated them, like right, justice, liberty, took on local, contradictory meanings. There had been so much speculation, by one side or the other, about their elasticity, that in the end they were reduced and extended to any old thing, to the point where they were made to say exactly the opposite of what they meant. Undoubtedly the military dictatorship profited from this destruction of semantic value, day by day more meticulous, a destruction which the most obtuse or cynically venal journalism took charge of. Those who, here and there, continued to worry about the real meanings, along with all that, connected to the emotions, can validly motivate mankind, were forced to remain silent, making it impossible to communicate amongst themselves or even to count themselves.

At a distance it is difficult, let me say again, to measure the extent of the damage that the war mentality has caused to the overall critical spirit. Nothing is more symptomatic of this than the acerbity of the debate over a recent work of small dimensions which has been distributed simultaneously in several countries: I am speaking of *The Silence of the Sea*, work signed with the pseudonym "Vercors" and presented as coming from the resistance movement in occupied France. Its innumerable readers immediately split into two opposing camps ready to come to blows at any pretext. One side sees in it, without room for discussion, a masterpiece: what's more, they applaud its invaluable effort to rise above the current conflict without ceasing to live through all its hardship, to recapture—without dwelling any more than necessary on their totally superficial and temporary eclipse—true human values. The others, no less passionate, denounce it as an unmistakable fake, a loathsome exploit of German propaganda, an incredibly perfidious device to undermine the morale of the Allies. While the ambiguity of the book's thesis and the interim impossibility of verifying its origins would demand an extreme prudence, the two sides have abandoned all equanimity when it comes to this subject. On both sides, the same failure of the critical faculty. Alternately exalted and reviled, the work leads a completely unhinged life, creating a deplorable precedent. In the judgments brought to bear on it, nothing which results from a careful examination of its methods, which rests on a comparison of its merits and its intrinsic weaknesses. The only thing taken into account is how it can be immediately useful or injurious. Who could be blind to the threat in introducing this manner of grappling with a work into the arena of artistic and literary free expression while giving complete license to such biases? If we don't watch out, who knows what obscurantism will spread imperceptibly to the works of the past?[1]

Nevertheless, where we were, we still are. And who can boast of having completely escaped the contagion, of proceeding through this fog any way but gropingly? Even space and time, which served as common points of reference, have been, under our very noses, stricken with discontinuity. Certainly, each person performs the mental operation of connecting the most widely separated countries by all the ancient and even future trade routes: it is no less true that these countries

---

[1] The author of *The Silence of the Sea* has revealed himself since then, destroying the suspicions of which he was the object and clearly demonstrating on which side lay the psychosis. But the core of this observation remains true (November, 1944).

have lived for a long time turned inward on themselves, half ignorant of what was being felt and experienced outside their borders. In Europe, in Africa, in Asia, states of awareness started out in little pockets well-isolated from each other. Masses of humanity, first in an orgy of conquest, bore down on other masses of humanity, at first infinitely suffering, who were able, for year and years, to maintain their resiliency, and who today rise again, bruised, while the former prepare to experience retaliation. But who can say, from a distance and undoubtedly even from close up, how the latter are rising again, who can comprehend the force of energy built up in them and, it must be said, the fatigue, too, once the first moment of enthusiasm has passed? It didn't take long to put up a bridge between the Paris of the beginning of 1940 and the Paris of 1944, but only a simplistic mind would maintain the illusion that those two Parises are the same. The great unknown is the current thinking of Paris and of some other European cities. That thinking has perhaps not yet been elucidated. Paris, its streets, its squares, according to the most recent evidence, are a total enigma: it's a question of knowing what tangible currents are already working to take over, what basis of differentiation, conforming to its unchanging complexion, it is in the midst of adopting, what lesson, as an organism obeying its own laws and not foreign orders, it will draw from its hard experience. Anything that tends to spread other views is only crude imagery. One must, in order to have an idea of the mechanism of assimilation and expulsion that it employs, know Paris well from the inside or, barring that, refer to certain masterful pages which Balzac devotes to it (except for the corrections necessitated by his social biases) like those which open *The Girl with the Golden Eyes.* It was essential that Paris liberate itself. Beyond that, one can only have complete confidence in its destiny, can only anticipate on the first auspicious occasion seeing it regain the unique physiognomy of its *heyday*. An immense shadow continues to spread over the world, owing to the voice of Paris not being heard and the eventuality, after a more or less long period of time, of a popular vote, supposing the impossible that it were without coercion or artifice, could not fill that gap, but instead a true and prolonged opinion poll in all domains, if sufficiently indicative eruptive phenomena do not happen on their own.

While I'm at it, I will use this parenthesis to explain a bit about the feelings my friends and I harbor with regard to what is French. A certain bent in our past declarations, which we were not afraid to make provocative, tended to convey the impression that we are completely breaking our ties with it, which would not fail to contradict the preceding. It is certain that, since the nineteenth century, some French poets and writers—Baudelaire, Rimbaud, Huysmans—began to batter with sarcasm "the French mind" or what already asserted itself as that in their time. Before going further, one might observe that their contribution to French-speaking culture more than compensates for whatever wrong they may have done, in France or in the world, to the mind in question, which is no more, all things considered, than *the dregs of that culture.* Without prejudice to the repugnance which art always feels at being placed in a national framework—art, which requires constant exchanges on the broadest plain—the extreme virulence which young writers indulge in when attacking "the French mind" and which reached a paroxysm between 1920 and 1930 leads one to think that that mind constituted then an obstacle and an intolerable menace which forced them to use all available weapons for their head-on attack. This is not very well understood abroad, where one is hypnotized by the almost limitless freedom of expression which France enjoyed during this period. It makes one lose sight of the lack of a vital response on the part of the immense majority of the public. In regard to art in particular—but the attitude towards art is likely to reflect all others—the reaction of public opinion is, in this period, terribly deceptive. It consists of boredom, of a profound sluggishness hidden under a mask of levity, of complacency, of the corniest commonplaces claiming to be good sense, of unenlightened skepticism, of "cageyness," all of which betray no other valid sentiment than a constant fear of being taken in. It's on account of this that it has continually been possible to hold a grudge against "the French mind," and I don't see how one can argue the fact that these features are real and hateful. If we have been resolutely contemptuous of that mind, isn't it to the extent that we wanted to awaken another one which the former was threatening more and more to sweep away, another one which, at intervals too far apart, displayed in France itself so much life, so much strength, including what that life and strength imply in the way of gravity, of the thirst for investigation and risk, of a driven dissatisfaction and still more of a generous *trust*, ineradicable, careful to remain open to all paths of human progress? I maintain that it is we who have shown ourselves to be the most loyal to that mind precisely to the extent that we didn't miss an opportunity to strike at the other, to corner it against what was shaky behind its feigned confidence and its forced smile. I say that in the true, the great French tradition, there is a mind which we have never ceased to lay claim to, to make our own: it's the one which winds through the Notebooks of the Estates General or which powers the decrees of '93, the one which, as self-interest fluctuates from one problem to another, inspires the Port-Royal movement as well as the *Encyclopédie*, which gives rise to Benjamin Constant and Stendahl just as, all through the last century it put its characteristic stamp on the worker's movement. Let no one see this as pleading in support of a humble petition on my behalf designed to shorten my time in exile. I remain convinced that when a people, even if it has been historically the greatest standard bearer of liberty in the world, idly waits for other peoples to reach its level, it will surely lose its genius and witness the decay of the ideas that give it substance only in retrospect. It is not only acceptable according to my lights, but it is then imperative that from its heart voices rise which will pester and exasperate it, accusing it without respite of having forfeited its mission.

The window, which had pivoted on its axis, carried far away and blurred by the images Baudelaire filled *Morning Twilight* with, returns and lands in front of me, then slowly unveils itself. More and more distinctly I begin to hear the voices of the two streams which were flowing at that allegorical end of the night. Left alone, I had almost stopped perceiving them or at least for me they had faded to a murmur. But I vaguely knew that this murmur is as indispensable to the continuation of life as the heartbeat. I didn't lose sight of the fact that it is not with dry legislation, with programs, with plans, with governments that one changes the world. The murmur has now given way to two clear, alternating voices. And this is what the streams say:

The left-hand stream.—I burn and I rouse, I carry out fire's bidding. The wind will never cease peeling misty rings off the trembling vase of fire I well from. And in this mist one can see through thin membranes the cities of the future. Not without great hesitation do they begin their upward motion and those that burst are always the most iridescent. In my perpetual boiling I can't help but cause the destruction of all living things, I'm devoted only to what threatens to fall lethargically to the earth's surface. I'm headed for that bleak pond where, under phosphorescent creams, ideas which have ceased to move men come to be buried. And this pond belongs to the dogmas that have met their end, to which men no longer make sacrifices except out of habit and pusillanimity. It belongs to the innumerable existences shut in on themselves, whose magma gives off, at certain times of day, a pestilential odor but who still retain the power to glitter with a new dream, because it is there that I bring the incessant bubbling of dissident ideas, of fermenting ideas and it's through me that it rediscovers in its depths the secret principle of its whirlpools.

The right-hand stream.—I bewitch and I multiply. I obey the freshness of water, capable of erecting its palace of mirrors in one drop and I'm heading for the earth which loves me, for the earth which couldn't fulfill the seed's promise without me. And the seed opens, and the plant rises, and the marvelous operation takes place by which a single seed produces several. And ideas would also cease to be fertile at the moment when man would no longer irrigate them with all that nature can individually instill in him in the way of clarity, mobility, generosity, and freshness of viewpoint. I bring to the soil where he walks that confidence he must have in the eternal greening of his reasons for hope at the very moment when they might appear to have been destroyed. I return intact the engine of his youth, the one which in better days, in the light of love, was able to make him believe he was the master of life.

The old pond no longer exists. The water got its ample breath back under the crook of the moon and below the crests of its waves it's dappled with every warm-water fish. Prominent among them are the purple and crow-blue "fighting fish" which can't stand each other's sight and are ready to battle their reflections to death. Their fencing is so lively that their glow remains behind them and wanders in all directions over the liquid and transparent shells, from the most supple to the most sparkling stroke. But the billows become calm, the single combat draws to a close or blossoms into a dawn, the two streams flow noiselessly, and from the earth, occupying the whole field of perception, rises the scent of a rose. Barely glimpsed a little while ago, the rose expresses in whiffs all of sacred Egypt in the trembling night. The rose is, vertiginously turned in on itself, the collar of the ibis, the sacred bird, and from it rise all the riggings that human dreams might need in order to recover on a tightrope and to make their white soles, split like the veins of leaves, glide again along the wire stretched between the stars. The rose says that the ability to regenerate is limitless, it shows that winter, with all its stains and severity, can never be considered more than transitory, better still, that its whips must periodically lash the roads to recall energy, to round up with their tips the thousand bees of energy who in the end will sleep in the too sensuous pomegranate of the sun.

The butterfly turns. During this last passage it remained still and facing front, mimicking a hatchet of light planted in the flower. A flutter now reveals its wing, thrice smattered with the dust of all precious stones. Its pump doesn't work any more, imponderable instruments developing from the flowery sap pause in the course of this barely material activity.

And, before taking flight to attend to the dissemination of the fecundating substance, before finding again the stippled and sinuous line that directs its flight, it only seems to exist in order to bring to the attention of our eyes the sumptuousness of that wing. And in its turn it tells what a consoling mystery there is in the raising of successive generations, what new blood incessantly circulates and, so that the species may not suffer from the wearing down of the individual, what selection always takes place just in time, succeeds in imposing its law despite all. Man sees this trembling wing which is, in all languages, the capital letter that begins the word Resurrection. Yes, the highest thoughts, the greatest sentiments can undergo a collective decline and the human heart can also break and books can age and all things must, on the outside, die, but a power that is not at all supernatural makes death itself the basis for renewal. To begin with, it guarantees all the exchanges which make sure that nothing precious is lost internally and that, through its obscure metamorphoses from season to season, the butterfly again puts on its exalted colors.

Still it's here that I invoke you because I'm aware that I can do no more till you appear, genies who secretly preside over this alchemy, you masters of the poetic life of things. This life is beyond the life of beings and very few are capable of understanding its reality, much less living it, although it constantly intrudes on the other. That other is made to be ground down, it is terribly exposed and fragile: it also happens that entire sections crack from it and that is never so true as when one loses without warning what one cherishes most in the world, made worse by the haunting enigma left when a life is struck down in its bloom. No greater cruelty enters our consciousness than this frightful void, following a fullness of heart without the slightest transition. In this state of instantaneous and total wreckage, it still rests on you, genies, to reach this heart, and without any of it transpiring outside or for its own sake, to get your alembics working on it. And if the operation you begin requires days and is paid for with the prism of tears, nevertheless the conjuring does still take place and life does end up, if not with a re-entry into grace, at least by being tolerable again. But then that life is not merely life blindly surrendered to and trusted in but rather life laden with all it can gather from the feeling of its concrete negation, it is a life which succeeds in continuing after having come full circle, life that has enlarged its domains to include regions inhabited by unforgettable beings who have left us and whose destiny, as opposed to our own, seems to be to maintain themselves at the zenith of what they were capable of being. In their full expanse, these regions are only explored by poetry, but undoubtedly, at this stage of my life, in order to transcend the great sorrow of these times and my own disarray and regain the poetic intelligence of the universe, eyes would have to open near me in which these regions were completely unveiled. Genies who make the water of those eyes so pure to me, I am far from having conveyed an impression of your power: to you belonged the marvelous task of making this complete giving of oneself survive its dearest love object, of making it lend itself to being useful, of reinstating itself somehow in life. Isn't the most admirable of your wiles, genies, to demand, in the very name of what no longer exists and we attached such value to, that beauty, grace, liveliness, all the resources of the heart and mind be safeguarded? You bring out the fact that their alteration, their diminution would stem from a sacrilegious consent. For the being whom even the enormity of regret cannot contain, but that would be the true, the unpardonable lapse of contact—to tell oneself: he wouldn't recognize me now!—that would be a deletion of the supreme hyphen. The most beautiful duty to him is to keep yourself the way he loved you.

That was for me the very key to the revelation which I spoke of and which I owed to you alone on the threshold of last winter. On the icy street I see you again modelled on a shiver, only your eyes uncovered. Your collar turned up, your hand pressing your scarf to your mouth, you were the very picture of secrecy, of one of nature's great secrets at the moment when it is surrendered and in your eyes of a storm ending one could make out the rising of a very pale rainbow. Since then, each time I've wanted to create for myself a physical image of the key, it's the structure of that eye which appeared to me under the very high shell scalloped by the left eyebrow, topped off by an imperceptible moon which allows it to stretch while tracing in its curve one or two undulations at the level of the pale crescent losing itself in the temple. This mysterious sign, which I've seen only in you, presides over a sort of palpitating question which simultaneously answers itself and always takes me back to the very source of spiritual life. From the connection between that look, still glittering with too many diamonds, and that bridge, sensitized as much as possible, under which it turns to pearl and slate and beneath the bird's wing worn smooth at the bend of that superb forehead, is constructed and balanced forever a moving face which right away became one for me with that key. That key radiates with such a light that one starts to worship the very fire in which it was forged. There is no triumph outside of that which, though allowed all the refinement of the knowledge of calamity, proves by its nature to be fundamentally a rebel against calamity itself. In this contradictory state of mind resides the most uncommon virtue which emanates from your being and which, without hesitation, I find myself designating with these words: "eternal youth," without having weighed them. It was enough just to see you to convince myself that eternal youth is not a myth. Its own seal conclusively marks for me that part of your face I've just so clumsily sketched. In fact there exists, among the elements which make it up, a relationship which henceforth all will be powerless to modify and the miracle is that such certainty is inherent in that relationship itself. This can no more be explained than a diamond. It's a star that is on you and which you must remain unaware of. All I can do is approximate its location. Moreover, the substance of this star is not organic: it is made from the radiance which spiritual life, brought to its highest degree of intensity, stamps on every expression of a human face.

The star reclaims its dominant position among the seven planets in the window whose fires grow dim to proclaim it the pure crystallization of night. In the only corner which still remained walled with darkness, the claws of a thousand lynx lacerated everything that obstructed vision, releasing a tree as they settle in along its branches whose foliage is such a fascinating green that it seemed to be made from the eyes of those same lynx. I wait for everything to return to its original serenity. The young woman continues to tilt her two vases over the ground and over the water, with her back to the thorny tree. But imperceptibly the scene is changing ... what's going on? the acacia comes so close it almost occupies the whole field of vision, doesn't it look as if its arms are pulling apart the window frames? Amazing! it's walking toward me, it's going to turn me upside down: I'm dreaming.

Ponds where suspicious stones emerge (among them perhaps some crocodile foreheads?). One of them pitches a pyramidal volume above the water and seems to float, to judge from the rag of seaweed suspended from its peak, whose rents take on hieroglyphic shapes in the wind. Its bevelled faces allow glimpses of bits of paint among which a green sun consumes itself, held up by scorpion stingers. All around it come feathers whirling as they land on the water; they are blue with rusty seedlings and they fall, alternating with drops of blood. Following these drops back to their source, one discovers way up in the sky the hawk's motionless oar and the hawk's eye scrutinizes the pond while in its heart a lamp is lit that allows us to see all that goes on in it. In this heart elaborately unfolds the mystery of memory and the future, and I, at that moment contemplating it, am the first to fear being blinded by it. Now the whole pond is turned upside down in the bird's eye, and what tears the bird apart is itself, because the depth of the pond is in it, and this depth then also becomes clear. In its aerial reflection the pyramid is restored to the whole it forms with its submerged base and this whole is a long sea chest which the bird's call reveals is hermetically enclosing some cherished remains. Nothing is more imperative to him than to continue to see this chest, for it to vie for his attention with the entanglements of weeds and the fury of the breakers. It's right then, at the most critical moment when he has just discovered it, just greeted the irretrievable with a cry of distress, that by attacking his own heart with his beak he only succeeds, to his supreme amazement, in enlarging it. In a spasm that contains the world's glory, this heart, while strangling on what was, reaches the abrupt limit where it swells to welcome at the peak of opposite exaltation, what will be. And in this heart of shadows opens at that moment a young heart of light, still completely dependent on the first one and demanding sustenance from it. It required nothing less than the vertigo of that abyss for blood to surge back through the canals of life. Ancient Egypt could not have created a better picture of the conditions surrounding the conception of a god.

Yet the chest slid down to the sea little by little. It got caught in the gears of its currents, it rolled endlessly in its tortuous glass staircases, it crashed against the doors of the topsy-turvy palaces explored by electric fish, then it was passed from hand to hand, raised higher and higher by liquid columns. And only then was it brought back to shore, stood bolt upright on land. And emotionally the earth is touched because nothing may ever profane it. The chest is there, hermetic as ever, bristling with the claws of barnacles and with its long mane streaming. But under it the soil is suddenly in turmoil: roots of an unknown force coil and uncoil till they seem to gather into themselves all the surplus energy of tropical rain forests and right before our eyes a tree grows from them to full maturity, and its lot is to enclose the chest within its trunk by nature's emergency decree. But I recognize this tree: it's the one that threw me to the ground a little while ago! now it has completely closed around its secret, and looks just as I first saw it. It doesn't differ in kind from the others surrounding it: it's only more noble than they. Here come some men wearing striped, light fabrics, carrying axes. They have orders to follow and they argue about them at length. They must be slaves. They finally choose the sacred tree. The tree trunk lying on the ground. Its cuts reveal flowery designs as in polished, petrified wood. The tree trunk at the studio of the king's sculptor. With each new attempt his chisel breaks, but the pillar which was ordered still magically springs up and it alone has the style that can consecrate a reign. The pillar set up in front of the king... But while they are preparing the celebration, all the rumors continue to revolve around the presence of a woman at court. Where have I seen that woman before? She is not without a vivid resemblance to the kneeling woman who held the urns, but her admirable body is now covered by a veil woven from stars and fastened with a moon at the junction of her thighs. Her hair, still uncoiled, supports a sparkling tiara of snakes and sheaves of grain and with her right hand she shakes a sistrum whose rhythm is picked up by her feet, miraculously exempt from prints. Whence and how she came, no one knows. The scribe only noted that her entry into the palace coincided with the disappearance of a swallow which was remarkable for its insistence on describing around the pillar, while it was being erected, some auspicious looking curves, but the account digresses to the point of attributing to her a series of spells: she doesn't care if she walks on land or on water, she perfumed the women in her entourage by breathing on them, in the absence of the wet-nurse she was seen suckling the royal infant with her finger. But the hour of her departure has already chimed and melancholy is also at the celebration. The queen's present is none other than the pillar that is slowly laid to bed using ropes. It now seems to have returned to its elemental nature: one could again start to count the sapwood rings. She who gets ready to take possession of it then begins the final preparations: she wraps in linen the trunk now more freshly cut than ever and lavishes on it odiferous balms whose scent spreads forever over the whole land.

A gap in the dream. Are we saying that nothing is ever found again? but that depressing certainty quickly summons another that compensates for it, more than that, it can reconcile the mind to the former, and that second certainty is that nothing is ever lost. The papyrus launch carries the goddess over all seas. But, do what she will, the adored body of he who was her brother and spouse will no longer flash before her eyes with its sovereign poise. She is condemned to reassemble the fourteen scattered pieces of that body which was the seat of infinite beauty and wisdom, and its mutilation will be even more implacable since the very organ for transmitting life has fallen prey to fish. Trembling, I'm witness to the sublime artifice possessing the means to carry out the enigmatic, inviolable law: what has been disassembled into fourteen pieces must be reassembled fourteen times. The wax and spices that will be used in this manifold re-creation are distributed among all the bits of divine debris that take up one corner of the studio, being one point of the two superimposed stars, one made of two equilateral triangles equal and secant to their parallel bases, the other of two equal and secant squares, each having two sides parallel to a diagonal of the other. I'm aware of the operation without being permitted to see it performed: blindfolded, I remain at the heart of the star with my compass. The fourteen perfectly identical gods are unveiled to me: the goddess will accompany them in the fourteen directions. To every priest waiting for one, each of the statues is presented as the only one and, assured that he alone possesses its truth and secret, he must promise under oath not to reveal what relic is contained in it. The masses gather in the temples around the rival statues. But throughout time, the more perspicacious glance of children can't tear itself away from the head at Memphis.

My turn to open my eyes. Green again, the acacia has reabsorbed the primitive figure while inside me the splendid myth unravels knots of meaning, at first so complex and many-levelled. How much richer, more ambitious and also more favorable for the mind it seems to me in that respect than the Christian myth! It's painful to observe how, under the latter's influence, the lofty interpretations that directed ancient beliefs have been continuously repressed. These beliefs have been systematically reduced to the *letter* of their contents: all that is retained is the poetic legend, generally agreed to be brilliant and it was thought possible to ascribe no other reference to them than the enumeration of the material needs of the peoples who shaped them. Thus the Philistine is satisfied to learn that Hopi ceremonies, exceptionally varied and requiring the intervention of the maximum number of supernatural beings the imagination can furnish faces and distinct attributes for, are intended more or less to lure every possible protection for the crops these Indian tribes cultivate, first among which is corn. Similarly, she whom the Egypt of the pharaohs held to be the queen of the heavens passes for having enjoyed no other prerogative in the minds of those who honored her than that of unleashing the floods of the Nile, eagerly awaited each year. Though it professes to be materialist, this positivist interpretation of myths, which only seeks to take account of the immediate and utilitarian, and carries simplification to the extreme, is no less insignificant. Who will accept that such elaborate constructs can be resolved and more or less exhausted by the analysis of the need to deify rain and other fertilizing elements required by arid lands? More inspiring and dignifying to the mind is the viewpoint of the mythographers themselves which emphasizes that in order for a myth to be viable, it must satisfy a number of meanings at once, among which we can distinguish the poetic meaning, the historical meaning, the uranographic meaning, and the cosmological meaning. The positivist interpretation, whose monopolistic and intolerant character I now denounce, can only pass for one branch of general historical interpretation, it alone already restricting ethnological interpretation, which stems from the same root. Without being able to follow the spiritualist path taken by any of the authors who have undertaken to come to terms with myths not from the outside but from within, and not being able, therefore, to accept the details of their classification, I must recognize that only this classification has so far proved to be broad enough to embrace the different sorts of outbreaks of a religious doctrine and to justify the persistent faith that may have been placed in it. Esotericism, with all due reservations about its basic principle, at least has the immense advantage of maintaining in a dynamic state the system of comparison, boundless in scope, available to man, which allows him to make connections linking objects that appear to be the farthest apart and partially unveils to him the mechanism of universal symbolism. The great poets of the last century understood this admirably, from Hugo, whose ties to the school of Fabre d'Olivet have recently been revealed; to Nerval, whose famous sonnets make reference to Pythagoras; to Swedenborg; to Baudelaire, who notably borrowed from the occultists their theory of "correspondences;" to Rimbaud, the nature of whose readings, at the apogee of his creative powers, one can't stress too much—it is sufficient to refer to the already published list of the works he borrowed from the Charleville library—right up to Apollinaire in whom the influence of the Hebrew Kabalah alternates with the novels of the Arthurian cycle of legends. With all due respect to certain minds who can only enjoy calm seas and light, in art this contact has not ceased and will not soon cease to be maintained. Conscious or not, the process of artistic discovery, if it remains foreign to the entirety of its metaphysical ambitions, owes no less fealty to the form and even the means of advancement of the highest magic. All the rest is indigence, is revolting, unbearable platitude: billboards and doggerel.

"Once," reports Eliphas Lévi, "the initiate of the Eleusinian mysteries had successfully undergone all the tests, once he had seen and touched holy things, if he was judged to be strong enough to bear the last and most terrifying of all secrets, a veiled priest ran towards him and tossed this enigmatic phrase in his ear: 'Osiris is a black god.'" Dark words more radiant than onyx! They are the ones which, when human questioning has been exhausted, seem to me the richest, the most charged with meaning. In this spiritual quest where every door one succeeds in opening leads to another door which one must exercise one's wits again to open, they alone, at the entrance to one of the last rooms, truly take on the shape of a pass key. But one must, in fact, in order to let them sink in, have stopped counting on the compass, have submerged oneself in the eccentric circles of the depths, have fixed in place—dear to my friend Marcel Duchamp—the "flying hearts" of bewilderment. It's there, at that poignant moment when the weight of endured suffering seems about to engulf everything, that the very excessiveness of the test causes *a change from a negative to a positive value*, tending to bring the inaccessibly human over to the side of the accessible and to imbue the latter with a grandeur which it couldn't have known without it,—that's where those words can be fully understood. One must go to the depths of human sorrow, discover its strange capacities, in order to salute the similarly limitless gift that makes life worth living. The one definitive disgrace one can bring upon oneself in the face of such sorrow, because it would make that conversion of signs impossible, would be to confront it with resignation. From whatever angle you noted the reactions that the worst evil you could conceive of left you open to, I always saw you put the heaviest accent on rebellion. There is, in fact, no more barefaced lie than the one that consists in asserting, even—and above all—when faced with an irretrievable situation, that rebellion is good for nothing. Rebellion is its own justification, completely independent of the chance it has to modify the state of affairs that gives rise to it. It's a spark in the wind, but a spark in search of a powder keg. I revere the dark fire that comes into your eyes whenever you are reminded of the unsurpassable wrong that was done to you and which is inflamed and clouded over again at the memory of the *miserable priests* who tried to approach you on that occasion. I also know that the very same fire raises its bright flames so high for my benefit, twines them into living chimeras before my eyes. And I know that the love which at this point counts on nothing but itself does not revive and that my love for you is reborn from the ashes of the sun. Also, each time a train of thought treacherously brings you back to the point where one day all hope was denied you and, at the precipice where you then stand, threatens, like an arrow seeking a wing, to hurl you again into the abyss, having experienced myself the vanity of all words of consolation and holding all attempts at distraction to be unworthy, I have convinced myself that only a magic spell could be effective here, but what spell could instill in itself and instantaneously give you the whole life force, life with all the intensity it can have, when I know that it came back to you so slowly? The one I decide to confine myself to, the only one I judge acceptable to call you back to me when it happens that you suddenly lean towards the opposite slope, consists in these words which, when you start to turn your head away, I just want to lightly brush your ear with: *Osiris is a black god.*

But the virtue of this spell goes well beyond the frame of individual life and extends over broad human units. I'm afraid that no other era than our own better lends itself to a demonstration of what I'm suggesting. No other, in fact, has succeeded in enlarging more, in elevating to a higher level the content of the word Resistance. All the most exalting and noble things that can be achieved, because not subservient to any external will, not subject to any limitations, and not shrinking from the sacrifice of one's own life—only then can one be sure that this sacrifice is voluntary—are commanded by this spirit of resistance as it is manifested in the occupied countries of Europe. Here all circumstances entitle us to speak of heroism, restore worth to a debased notion. I was thinking about this a few days ago while looking at a photograph of a French journalist, Pierre Brossolette, who formerly headed the foreign affairs desk at *Populaire*, and whose death in a Paris hospital was noted in a Canadian paper. My eyes went back and forth from this young and smiling face to the few lines that accompanied it, which described how Brossolette had just succumbed to the effects of horrible wounds incurred in the course of his struggle in the underground. Between these two documents, the news item and the picture, there was a contradiction which, though it made the information more dramatic, tended to resolve itself, as paradoxical as this might be, all to the benefit of trust and life. The last word, how to put this? belonged to that swaggering and deliberately skeptical expression which just a bit of very Parisian bravado seemed to slip into. That man must have been one of those who knows how to see beyond himself, who knows at what point life is not worth living, who freely and without hesitation knows how *to take a risk.* One of those who knows how to die, just as they knew how to live. Faced with the disappearance of such beings, in such a battle, human pride vies with affliction and the lead keeps changing hands. *Osiris is a black god.* If I only make one man the model here, understand that it is in order to command all the power of the *concrete,* but implied in this homage are vast groupings, as they are organized in all the invaded countries. Nevertheless, one scruple demands our attention here. From a distance, it is at least possible to presume that the spirit of resistance taken in the broadest possible sense and whose unselfishness I right away put beyond question, will not be as clearly illuminated for everyone as it has been for some. Today the word resistance is as if brand new, it has been so thoroughly rejuvenated that it is considered, no doubt very imprudently, exempt from the wear and tear affecting the fabric of vocabulary: one is completely dazzled at having discovered a new virtue, without even making the effort to observe that it is not one that is numbered among the "Christian virtues," and that it is unlikely, in the final analysis, to be reconciled with certain of the latter. But, however admirable and necessary it was as a spontaneous phenomenon, the will to resist cannot be considered for long outside the context of what motivated it in one person or another and it might be worthwhile, in this respect, to guard against disillusion. It is probable that the reaction of the masses, in the area where they are least conscious—with the exception of the working class—was completely instinctual and was fixed on no other objective than to bring an end to an intolerable oppression whose effects were immediately felt in their very flesh. This almost chemical phenomenon of rejection eventually found its counterpart and its moral justification only within the framework of patriotism. It goes without saying that once the yoke has been removed, these elements risk falling back into their previous errors, dashing back into pursuit of completely egotistical well-being, simply heightening their position of aggressive defiance towards all who don't speak the same language they do. Next to this thoroughly episodic and terribly limited form of resistance sits the truly conscious form, where the real question is one of knowing to what extent it has succeeded in educating the former and maintaining it in a state of alert and readiness. It's the one that, beyond the most urgent task of concentrating everything towards this objective: repel the invader, works at determining the underlying causes of the current conflict and off every beaten path—as far as the eye can see prey to the same ambushes—prepares the radical measures which alone can prevent his return. Rid the air of those abject clouds of locusts, set free the most fundamental right to live from the extreme limitations that a manifestly parasitic interference imposes on it, cleanse the sites exposed to the contamination of repression by all those who accommodated themselves to the claw on the nape, we can imagine, once again, nothing more essential, and still that does not yet constitute a decisive step towards a world forever sheltered from what just infested it. The necessary, what must without contest take urgent precedence over all the rest, is still quite far from being sufficient. In the interval that separated this war from the last, the concept of liberty, which shone brilliantly and with extraordinary prestige in the days of the French Revolution, was in France itself in the process of being disregarded or lost. Everything that allowed the genius of a people to assert itself bent more and more under the pressure of hostile forces, more or less disguised. Whatever could have been added to its assets—the fundamental code of this people as, like it or not, it arose from its institutions—was left in the shadows out of fear that the concept of liberty, which doesn't take well to resting, might become more demanding. Its already ancient conquests were no longer recited except for memory's sake, with all sorts of cautions and reservations, so that the recollection of it should be as little uplifting as possible. What's worse, they always seemed to apologize for it as if it were a childhood disease which had endangered the life of the patient—this very people—but was happily treated in time by such eminent practitioners as Corday, Tallien, Napoleon Bonaparte, or Monsieur Thiers. Obviously, there were grounds for even the most faint-hearted to be reassured. May the recent events have taught France and the world that liberty can only subsist in a dynamic state, that it becomes denatured and negates itself at the moment when one makes of it a museum piece. But enough of this Byzantine discussion of its nature: it would not only be futile but actually perilous to begin a fundamental debate about liberty in which everyone with an interest in muddling the issue would rush to participate. Having deliberately put aside its philosophical import, which doesn't concern us here, but which its adversaries know how to use to their advantage in order to obscure it, liberty can be quite well defined by contrast with all forms of servitude and constraint. The one weakness of this definition is that it generally represents liberty as a *state*, that is, as immobile, although all of human experience demonstrates that such immobility brings about its immediate ruin. Humanity's aspirations for liberty must always be given the power to recreate themselves endlessly; that's why it must be thought of not as a state but as a *living force* bringing about continual progress. Besides, that is the only way in which it can continue to oppose constraint and servitude, which themselves are continually recreated in the most ingenious fashion. Let us beware: for the prisoner, liberty is a wonderfully concrete thing, positive as long as it is beyond the bars, but in the full daylight of the outside the joys he anticipated from it can be so quickly exhausted! Once the first moment of relief and excitement has passed, he will make use of that liberty without truly enjoying it—just as we no longer experience the delight of living in peace with our teeth once the crises of our early years are past!—and even more so if right away, worrying, he doesn't ask himself what to do with that liberty. Unfortunately, this is the risk faced by all those in the resistance movement in France and elsewhere who limit their objective to liberating territory. The effort of liberation only coincides in a partial and fortuitous manner with the struggle for liberty. A quite formal distinction between these two terms is imperative today when some are preparing to take advantage of this confusion to the detriment of liberty. The concept of liberation has the disadvantage of being a negative concept, of having only momentary value and only in relation to an actual and sharply defined plundering that must be stopped. These kinds of concepts, in themselves not constructive—we saw this clearly with pre-war anti-fascism, mired in the rut of pure opposition—are born short-sighted. The concept of liberty, on the other hand, is a concept completely in control of its destiny, which reflects an unconditional view of what *denominates* a human being and it alone gives an appreciable meaning to human *growth*. Liberty is not, like liberation, a struggle against sickness, it is *health*. Liberation might make us believe that health has been recovered, though it only signifies a remission of the illness, the disappearance of its most obvious and alarming symptom. Liberty itself eludes all happenstance. Liberty, not just as an ideal but as a constant recreator of energy, in the way that it existed in certain people and in the way that it provides a model for us all, must rule out any idea of comfortable equilibrium and conceive of itself as constant *erethism*. The primordial need for liberation, which has just been very widely felt, and love of liberty—one can't hide the fact that this remains much more a matter of choice—owing to the severity of these times have had an opportunity to walk side by side. Better still, they were measured by the same rule which is courage, *true* courage, requiring the *free* acceptance of danger. It is no less fervently to be wished that once the last hussar has been expelled and put out of harm's way and the last traitor has been shot, that none of those who took on the best of them in the most one-sided battle possible will believe themselves capable of stopping there. In the very heart of whatever stirs him, if his thoughts should turn ever so slightly inward, he will discover the actual spark of that liberty which asks only to grow larger and to become a burning star *for everyone.* I say they will see that liberty dawning and they will merely have to *remember* and right before their eyes, in the future, even the worst intentioned will give up splitting hairs, and know to what extent their ideas are only intellectually based, just as history is, and even the most reactionary and biased mind will refrain from calling to account the soldiers of Valmy.

The star found here again is the early morning star, which tended to eclipse the other heavenly bodies in the window. It surrenders to me the secret of its structure, explains to me why it numbers twice as many points as they, why its points are fiery red and yellow, as if it were two overlapping stars with alternating rays. It is the product of the actual unity of these two mysteries: love summoned to rebirth from the loss of the love object and only then rising to its full consciousness, to its complete dignity; liberty vowing to really know itself well and to become dynamic since its own loss is at stake. In the nocturnal image that was my guide, the resolution of this double contradiction takes place under the protection of the tree that encloses the remnants of dead wisdom, through exchanges between the butterfly and the flower and by virtue of the principle of the uninterrupted expansion of fluids, connected to the certainty of eternal renewal. Besides, this resolution is a shared one, needing only the documentation that the ancient Hebrews hieroglyphically represented by the letter פ (pronounced: *phay*) which resembles the tongue in the mouth and which means the word itself in its highest sense.

Nevertheless, the allegorical truth expressed here seems to me only capable of expanding to its fullest extent when it is completed and clarified by an adventitious myth. In fact, a certain lack of information continues to exist concerning the circumstances that govern, in the image I retraced, the appearance of the primary star and which could eventually permit us to reach its source. Now, this gap can be filled in. There exists, in fact, on the walls of time, a picture very similar to the previous one in regard to the nature of the preoccupations it betrays and which undoubtedly has only escaped being compared to it earlier because of extreme differences in their workmanship. This picture, whose subject is the formation of the star itself, constitutes in my eyes the supreme expression of Romantic thought, in any case it remains the most lively symbol it has bequeathed to us. This is the symbol that Monsieur Auguste Viatte has played a great part in shedding light on in his recent work: *Victor Hugo et les Illuminés de son temps* and which emerges from a parallel between *The Testament of Liberty* by the Abbé Constant, published in 1845, and *The Last of Satan*, one of the poet's last lyric works. "As with Victor Hugo," writes Monsieur Viatte, "we are, with the Abbé Constant, first witness to the fall of the angel who, at birth, refused to be a slave," and who pulled behind him into the night "a shower of suns and stars through the magnetism of his glory;" but Lucifer, the outlaw intellect, begets two sisters, Poetry and Liberty and "the spirit of love will borrow their features to subdue and save the rebel angel." This account, necessarily quick and dry, doesn't at all prepare us—for he who, braving the other extreme, agrees to go beyond verbal incontinence—for the grandeur that Hugo's visionary gift bestows on such an episode and of which his creation of the angel of Liberty is the particular evidence in his work: "The angel of Liberty, born from a white feather shed by Lucifer during his fall, penetrates the darkness; the star she wears on her forehead grows larger, becomes, 'first meteor, then comet and furnace.'" We see how, where it may once have been unclear, the image sharpens: it's rebellion itself, rebellion alone is the creator of light. And this light can only be known by way of three paths: poetry, liberty, and love, which should inspire the same zeal and converge to form the very cup of eternal youth, at the least explored and most illuminable spot in the human heart.

August 20 – October 20, 1944.
Percé – Sainte-Agathe.

APERTURES

Already this book, which from a certain viewpoint gives the impression of wanting to clarify a liqueur even though that liqueur is not yet free of some of the reactions that clouded it, is unreasonably attempting nothing less than to shape and polish in a way which still retains the casting marks, has not been able to avoid substantial contradiction by time, has revealed at this or that angle what in it might have been fallible. Three springs, in particular, have sufficed to lead us to feel the greatest fear for the vitality of the young tree of the Resistance, which at the end of a particularly cold and clammy night seemed to shoot up from the earth as if pushed, and with a potential for an equally unstoppable power to grow. This Resistance, for those who hailed it then as I did, was considered to be the product of a need that exceeded in all ways its immediate justification—a need finally possessing the means to manifest itself in life and to satisfy itself. It's true our eyes are not slow to be dazzled when they slowly gaze on the phenomenon of germination. This need I speak of was, in this case, like the acorn of the oak which, this was not to be fortuitous, made a Claude de Saint-Martin find his greatest strains, as well as a Fabre d'Olivet. I'll limit myself to recalling that, for the former, the emanation of the oak, born—as is the child—in the temporal realm, manifests the transcendental design of all beings "to regain their resemblance to their source"[1] and that in the eyes of the latter the acorn undergoing the process of germination expresses the reconciliation of the "force of being" which he also calls "providence," with the force of being what it is, or the force of existing as an oak, which he calls "destiny," these two forces occasionally being subordinated to a third, which is "man's will." And Fabre d'Olivet explains himself as concretely as possible on this point: "I hold the acorn, I may eat it and thus assimilate it into my substance; I may give it to an animal who will eat it; I may destroy it by crushing it underfoot; I may plant it, and cause it to produce an oak ... I crush it underfoot: the acorn is destroyed. Has its destiny been obliterated? No, it is changed; a new destiny, which is my work, begins for it." [2] These last sentences might tend to drag us down a melancholy slope. The spirit of resistance, with all that it entails in the way of openness, generosity, liveliness, and audacity, isn't it brutally botched here? A little quick calculation of the current situation is enough to make one believe it—from the recent Indochina massacres and the "lines" constantly stretching out the doors of Paris bakeries, all that which (in another context) has come around to pinning the labels lie and mockery on the so-called "aims of war"—to the even more somber certainty, that no spontaneous current of significant breadth espouses the fundamental reservations set forth on page 47 of this book which, after Bacon, Condillac, and Fourier, lead us to conclude that we must "remake human understanding."

All things taken into account, it certainly seems that the arrested development followed by the rapid withering of the organism that concerns us here need not at all be explained by an extrinsic cause contrary, perhaps, to the destruction of the acorn by the human foot. Before blaming an unfavorable terrain or climate, it would be appropriate to verify first whether the organism was afflicted by any constitutional vice? Was there a worm in the fruit or did a caterpillar attack the very first sprouts? It's only too obvious. Whatever the case, this larva has a name: it's called nationalism.

1   Claude de Saint-Martin: *Tableau naturel.*
2   Fabre d'Olivet: *Histoire philosophique de genre humain.*

One of the weaknesses of Arcanum 17 *was to have not sufficiently warned against its ravages, to have not foreseen that it threatened, from top to bottom, minds that I wanted to believe were steeped in its very negation.*[1]

The very exacerbation of nationalist feeling among those who had shown themselves to be the most violently contemptuous of it authorizes me, I freely admit it, to call to account for certain waverings (I hope less real than it would appear) those who share my concern for the integrity of thought. It's true I didn't take all the necessary precautions to shelter from equivocality the contents of the parenthesis which opens on page 73 and which momentarily alarmed certain of my friends whose esteem is dear to my heart. Nonetheless, one mustn't forget that my words arrive here transatlantically, that is, from

---

1   From certain people's earlier declarations, sufficiently well publicized, one can perhaps brave bad taste to sample these, towards the day when contrived passions will finally declare a truce, granting humanity the luxury to *appreciate:*

"It's funny. My great-grandfather Eluard was a soldier for fourteen years during the conquest of Algeria: seven years for himself and seven years to buy his brother out of the service. My father was a soldier for six years. Six years for me, too; with the years of the Occupation, ten. We're from military families. Military poets...."

"... Poetry which forbids itself certain themes is inferior poetry. I used to hate the word 'Kraut' since it seemed to me disloyal. I don't hate it any more."

(Paul Eluard, interviewed by Paul Guth, *La Gazette des Lettres*, February 2, 1946.)

"... We still have in our midst today Abel Bonnards who will only take off their masks when an enemy puts his foot back on the neck of the fatherland, and defeatists when it comes to national pride, as Giono was, and it matters little to me if they come from the Right or the Left! since they want to yank the hands of the French away from their work, prevent the miner from quarrying the coal or the printer from pulling the newspaper, they are my enemies, they are France's enemies."

Aragon (Speech given during the National Convention of the National Union of Intellectuals, February 24, 1946.)

a continent where they take the easy way out by differentiating, even if only by external behavior, the various types of Europeans without making any hierarchical distinctions among them. It seemed to me, and it still seems to me, that to praise what I see as the "pluses" of the French mind (in contrast, though, to serious irregularities and defects capable, for the time being, of passing for latent) for the same reason that, right from the opening pages of Arcanum 17, I speak highly of the Italian, English, German, or Russian contribution where I esteem we are universally indebted to them, did not imply on my part any attribution of unrivalled merit to the word "France." If I lost my way for a moment it was, I concede, because I gave in to polemical fervor which makes one, however slightly, lose control of one's words; so I spoke of a "real" tradition in contrast to another which since then has not turned out to be at all viable. I have also been candid in admitting, without reservation and according to undoubtedly premature and biased information, that Paris had succeeded in finding in itself forces sufficient to liberate itself.

Out of a desire to assuage the worries mentioned just above but also to demonstrate that I don't believe I need to indulge in any more serious repentances, I will permit myself to refer to my lecture to the students at Yale (The Situation of Surrealism Between the Two Wars, 1942)[1] and I'm reproducing here this practically unknown text (in its first version disfigured by misprints) dating from May, 1943, which I published in the second issue of Monde libre without—I believe—having sacrificed too much to the official tone of the magazine that asked me for it:

1   Editions Fontaine, 1945.

BLACK LIGHT

P ARDON ME for haggling over my offering to you, insatiable god of war. I know how much is given to you these days and that you no longer even have to bend over to pick *it* up. But what if I still dared to speak of what's denied you? Once more you're there, haggard, foul, smashing your big blue toys as one follows right after the next, ever more numerous, more perfect, in a cloud of flies. You take advantage of this to make people say that having always existed, you will always exist and I concede that nothing works more in your favor than the philosophy of the "eternal return" where the final word can only be "what's the point?" Nevertheless you do not impress me with your presence and your virulence, so little, in fact, I suspect that the secret of your definitive suppression is within the reach of man, who has well known how to exorcise plague or rabies. For the time being, circumstances would have it that we are hardly permitted to dream of it: evil is too huge, presses much too close to us, we can only confront it at the moment when all hope of a preventative cure has receded.

The time will come again when man, having put war behind him, must at all costs convince himself it need not necessarily reappear in front of him. There will be no such thing as being too energetic in repressing the schemes of fatalism and skepticism, not to mention cynicism, and still it will be necessary beforehand to deprive those who pride themselves on such attitudes of the benefits of wealth or others they aspire to, without which, of course, there would *in fact be nothing.* Historical task worthy of the best but the initiation and forms of it also depend on how the situation unfolds subsequent to the current war and can just barely be conjectured.

Aside from all expectations in this realm, war, as a phenomenon we are witness to, lends itself to many observations that can be of great interest later on. If it tends to be taken for the ultimate form of resolution invoked by certain conflicts among peoples, it is undeniable that it covers up a very complex aggregate of more or less similar individual impulses which seek in it their fulfillment. The conscience of mankind has always managed poorly when it has believed it can make war just. It is not enough, to have done with it, to remove its primary cause. If all of humanity can be likened to one body, who would maintain that one can expect relief from its ills from a generalized archaic "bloodletting?" And who doesn't feel the wrenching war gives to the very notion of *right* (which it is all too easy to subjectify and to exalt contradictorily in each camp) seeing that, threatened with brute force, it must itself appeal to brute force, and thus partially give in to it? *A priori* these few insights uproot any mental compliance with the idea of war. In order to perpetuate itself up to our times with, if not the assent, at least the resignation of mankind, it must conceal such shady means of seduction.

Preventing the return of war cannot seriously be discussed

until we have taken pains to consider not its more or less obvious ends, but the means it sets in motion; not its unthinkable justifications, but its *structure.*

I'm not hiding the fact that this leaves us open to bitter reflections, but I think we can bear the weight if that is the price for more clairvoyance, even more so if we are convinced that the cure can only be born from a less superficial understanding of the illness.

We must begin by taking away from war its letters patent of nobility. And let me make myself clear here: within the abominable framework of war there has been a great show of grandeur. This grandeur, when it is *true* grandeur, only demonstrates in a stagey way, the measure of certain men. In less inclement weather, their outlay of generosity might be the same, and all things considered, less vain. Military heroism presents at least this other side of the coin, that in the midst of battle one must sometimes also accord it to one's adversary, which leads one to value not only different parts, but the most gungho and undoubtedly the most responsible ones, of a *whole* one professes to abhor. This above all is the trouble spot at the heart of the many lines of interference which run through war and whose network represents the cruelest possible emotional ambivalence in mankind.[1]

---

1 Let us beware of extremist simplifications which benefit war and which can create in their wake the most serious disappointments. There is no point in concealing from ourselves, for instance, the fact that common hopes and interests are not enough, are not sufficient, from a psychological and moral standpoint, to unify fully the spirit of the front and the rear, more broadly speaking the zones that suffer and the zones that remain intact. Between them stretches, despite everything, the gap that separates the most acute, the most dramatic and all-encompassing perception from mental represen-

Differences in ideals which set one nation against another, one group of nations against another group, may be strong enough to provoke or lighten the sacrifice of millions of beings, and while they theoretically motivate wars, belong nonetheless to the *superstructure.* Within this functions a system that brings into conflict not only the "ego" and the "id" as Freud would term it, but also, within the bounds of races, States, regimes, castes, beliefs, an "us" (organic or purely conventional?) which behaves like a hybrid of the two. This restrictive *us*, bristling with all the quills of the "superego" (or *ego ideal*), in addition to, it certainly seems, a few other things, complicates and denatures life to such an extent that everything must be done to dissolve it in the *everyone*, with mankind as the only unconditional rallying cry.

One of the newest facets of this war, openly expressing itself on the side opposing our own, is the hunger of war for war. Fascism is not afraid to label it the height of mental health. There it was, around 1910, a lucky find of Italian Futurism, apparently born of the grossest advertising cacophonies but which nevertheless provided a basis of codification for the theoreticians of National Socialism, whose prototype remains Ernst Jünger: "In discord and in war, when man rips up all conventions and all treaties, which are only a beggar's patchwork rags, bestiality rises from the depths of the soul like a

---

tations which, even aided by photographic and other reports, remain more or less weak and leave an enormous margin for thoughtlessness, for distraction. It is better to see this gap to avoid its being dug, once more, in hindsight. After 1918 one was occasionally surprised to witness the beginnings of effusiveness between former military enemies, for want of something better, reconciled in a certain contempt for others and in a nostalgia for the days when they were tearing each other to shreds.

mysterious monster... The voluptuousness of blood floats over war like a red sail on a dark galley."[1] An atrocious mysticism, which we must nevertheless delve into if it's true that we are struggling today to rid the world of it. Could Jünger's form be so lyrical, despite being at the service of erroneous, not to mention criminal content, without grasping one of the great moments of human despair? Here it's *error*, the conquering worm, which we must expose at the center of the beautiful fruit.

Is it true, or rather will it be certain tomorrow that this error is particularly, exclusively German? I concur that one can find in this vestiges of myth such as the one about the Young Man-Beasts from ancient Germania. But still... On the afternoon when war was to have been declared in France, from a window which looked out on the interior courtyard of Fort Nogent, I observed the action below. It had just been announced over the radio that hostilities would begin at five o'clock. Impossible to recognize in those troops the emotion one would imagine such news would evoke. Truly lacking any tangible reaction on the scale of the event, at first it was only a vague cheerfulness which increased as time passed. Only an hour left, five minutes. As the uproar mounted, the abundance of contortions suggested a school recess. In the corners, the least newly-arrived, those who had put their fatigues on again the night before, became feverish over their Pinochle, which opened up endlessly repeating vistas. Faced with such a scatterbrained spectacle, the doctor I was leaning next to, I'd still call him a pretty tough guy, began to cry. As for the others'

---

1 Ernst Jünger: *La guerre notre mère* (excerpted in *"Lettres françaises,"* number 5; July, 1942).

euphoria, baffling at first glance, it's not enough to deplore it, one must discover its causes and, if you ask me, I wouldn't hesitate to point the finger at the platitudes and constraints of civilian life in peacetime. That life, for the most part, is limited, more or less unconsciously, by having to hold down a job they didn't choose, by the troubles of family guardianship or the worries of a home their hearts do not burn brightly for, all of which sap their self-determination, but, even more so, by the *boredom* of going again today almost exactly where they went yesterday. The immense practical advantage war derives from this very common form of dissatisfaction leads one to think that, to avoid future wars, it is all those who create this dissatisfaction itself whom one must first radically attack on a universal scale.

We are not concerned here with formulating the means by which many will cease to find in war an escape from what is monotonous and oppressive in their individual existences. And besides, it might be premature to divulge these means. Nevertheless, one must allow that from now on *plans* must be drawn up for this eventuality and stored in a safe place. The quality most demanded of them would be extreme audacity.

And first of all, man's terrible need for enduring infancy cries out to be satisfied. Take yourself back to that extremely upsetting episode in the film *Victory in the Desert:* we've just seen, for the last hour, what was the inferno of Libya. Now the Italian prisoners, exhausted, both physically and psychologically broken, march away, innumerable. But one of them has just spotted the camera and all those around him look back. *They're going to be in the movies!* Who will see them? Friends or enemies? they don't even wonder, and *smile.* Elsewhere, no doubt other prisoners, in a similar situation, also smiled.

This compensating mechanism which, in the extremity of

suffering, can make one seek out the most innocent, the most empty pleasure, is captured alive there. We're on the track of those paradoxical affective reactions described in dementia praecox. Outside of pathology and of course without prejudice to the brilliant feats of arms which abound in wars in order to win our hearts, the moral misery of this period is infinite.

Only when we seize it by the scruff of the neck will we really have done with the immemorial wrath of demons called petroleum or saltpeter.

Human life must be *reimpassioned*, rendered valuable again, if necessary from the point of view of that which, quite realistically for each of us, is given to us only once. Perhaps in consequence of this it must be allowed a completely different latitude. May Arab story tellers of the streets, now enjoying an unaccustomed popularity, create one day soon imitators in our American and European squares. And may imagination everywhere, so shamefully channelled, run its course! May festivals, where each will play an active role, be broadly enough conceived to periodically exhaust all the phosphorescent power contained in mankind. In our youth such an impulse was expressed on certain Bastille Day evenings, on certain May Day mornings when, despite the increasing vigilance of window-closers, a whiff of liberty intermittently wafted by.

All efforts to reorder the world through economics, as much as they are of prime importance in my eyes, will sooner or later fall short if one doesn't take into account this appetite for curiosity, for pomp, and above all for more individual opportunity to roam around existence. A painter friend of mine writes me from Mexico that he couldn't resist the temptation to see a volcano erupt a week earlier in the area around Uruapan. The birth of this volcano was announced by about three hundred tremors. From a crater now one hundred and fifty meters high, it spits, in the midst of superb Matta-style flames, boulders as big as houses. "There is," adds my friend, "an explosion about once every seven seconds, accompanied by tremors." But what is most interesting in his letter is that he was struck by the contentment, based on pride, of those he encountered along the way. A new volcano, and so gifted, right near us! It's true that the Indian peasants, in this village of Ajuno as in others, are frustrated in every direction. What would you have to convey to them, not to mention give them, to make them leave their volcano without regrets?

For today, I wanted to invite meditation only on this most neglected side of the problem of the *infrastructure*. As for me, I remain faithful to the conviction that action, even in the rigorous and unquestioned form it takes today for those who fight in the name of liberty, will only be valuable so long as our interpretation of the world, at the same time, will not have the brakes slammed on it, that is to say that one continues to seek to know, without absurd illusions, what this liberty might consist of. Everything else is obscurantism, and like it or not, pro-fascism.[1] In view of the solutions that are asked of us, routine, completely upholstered in velvet, is more dangerous, routine hatches more distress and death than an imaginary utopia. Faced with the total bankruptcy of our pre-

---

[1] This is the only effective defense one can hope to make against this additional peril, and perhaps the most serious one: led by necessity, against one's interests, to commit day after day a series of acts in all manner similar to those of the enemy, how will we avoid pitching camp with him when we reach a mutual limit? Beware: by the very fact that we are obligated to adopt this means, we risk being contaminated by what we believe we are defeating.

conceived ideas, it would be best to give free reign of expression, public or not, to the latter. A young woman, beautiful and lost in one of those prophetic-looking daydreams that are dear to my heart, said to me the other day: "You see, right now we shouldn't say anything hard. What's the *opposite* of hard? Everything we have the right to set down on paper, and from time to time, that's still a poem. Today we have to make cloudy children. You understand, not children made of clouds, but children with cloud parts, yes: cloudy children."

II

Of Isis, who has just promised the Golden Ass to restore his human form, Apuleius splendidly says that, "she withdrew into herself."

I wrote in 1933: "Perception and [mental] visualization—which seem to the ordinary adult to be so radically opposed—should only be considered products of the dissociation of a single original faculty... *traces of which exist in the primitive and in the child. This state of grace is what all those concerned with defining the true human condition more or less confusedly aspire to rediscover... One can systematically, safe from all delirium, work stripping the necessity and value from the distinction between the subjective and objective.[1] The quest for such a "state of grace," to which, moreover, at the end of this text, no other name but* ecstasy *is given (Teresa of Avila, mediums), has not, since then, ceased to be for me the supreme alternative to a life devoid of meaning so long as it remains slave to the idea of a* denatured *world. Nevertheless, like many others, on an intuitive impulse I opted in love for the passional and exclusive form, tending to*

[1]   "Le message automatique," (*Point du jour*, N.R.F., pub.).

proscribe along with it all that could be accounted for as compromise, whimsy, and straying from the path. I know that this view has perhaps seemed narrow and arbitrarily limiting and for a long time it's been difficult for me to defend it reasonably when it happened to collide with those of sceptics or even more or less avowed libertines. A remarkable thing, I've been able to verify a posteriori that the majority of quarrels that cropped up in surrealism where political differences were used as a pretext were overdetermined not, as some have insinuated, by personal questions, but by an irreducible disagreement on this point. There was bound to be—whether or not we forgot about it while on one level we were on the same road—an increasing distance among us as we went through life, which threatened to separate us on another level. This "state of grace," depending on whether one chooses at the outset to head towards it on the broken and perilous trail belonging to it or if one prefers to this—without asking where they lead—the agreeably shaded paths, remains in effect the great divider and distributor of human luck. For those who, once and for all, have put their chips on it or against it, it doesn't give second chances. "Love," says Michelet, "is a very high and noble thing in a woman; she bets her life on it." Nothing can long unite in mutual comprehension the man who makes the same bet on love and he who objects to the risk. I say today with complete certainty that this state of grace results from the reconciliation in one single being of everything that can be expected from without and from within, that it exists at that one instant in the act of love when exaltation at the peak of the senses' pleasure is no longer distinguishable from the lightning realization of all the mind's aspirations. Anything short of this can in no way lay claim to the name love but in fact arises from the worst complacency towards what we, the surrealists, have taken as our task to combat, gives advance warning of a spiritual resignation whose other facets will not be long in manifesting themselves. I say that what causes the reconciliation of physical perception and mental visualization is one and that it is out of the question, in the realm of love, to haggle over what one is ready to concede in the realm of expression. To the extent that surrealism does not deny itself the right to judge without niceties poetry or *painting that continues, right up to the present, to call solely on either a sensory or intellectual stimulus, it is proper that in its very heart it deal no less strictly with that sort of* irreparable *frivolity. The surrealist way can only be identical in these two cases. The act of love, just as with a painting or a poem, is discredited if he who surrenders to it does not do so in a* trance.

There eternity, as nowhere else, is seized in the very moment. The trembling lunar mirror reappears on the forehead of night crowned with sheaves of grain and with tuberoses, lighting up only the divine face and breast combined by the whirling helices of blond or blue ringlets in the summer wind. The ibis, the jackal, the vulture, and the snake, assisted by Nephthys, await only a sign. The imperishable secret is once more written in the sand.

III

My friends Jacques Hérold, Victor Brauner and I had agreed that last Sunday afternoon, April 27, we would climb to the top of the Saint-Jacques Tower together. The idea for this project came to us a few days earlier as I finished telling them the story of an enigmatic adventure which happened to a young painter who let me in on it—Jacques Halpern, whom I met only recently but whom I consider exceptionally inspired. In order to lose nothing of the atmosphere emanating from this adventure, I'll endeavor again to reproduce his actual words:

"As I was leaving my house that day"—he lives where the Boulevard Sébastopol starts—*"I took, contrary to habit, the Rue des Lombards and turned at the corner of the Rue Saint-Denis.*

"I was crossing the Rue de Rivoli when my glance was arrested by the Saint-Jacques Tower (living near this monument I generally don't pay much attention to it.) The words Saint-Jacques Tower *followed me to the edge of the Place du Châtelet where, again, I was surprised to find myself staring intently at the number of the bus turning onto the Rue Saint-Denis: it was the 21. At that moment the clock at the Ministry of Justice rang* three.

"The impossibility of ignoring this stemmed from the seemingly urgent structure of these elements:

"The Saint-Jacques Tower, the 21st, 3 o'clock.

"*That had the air of a message (as soon as I became aware of it the anxiety I was experiencing up till then gave way to a pleasant, relaxed sensation). My thoughts often went back to that day and in the days that followed I could only free myself from my obsession with it by crediting it with being a rendezvous. The wishing and waiting for the appointed day were marked by lightning jolts separated by long intervals.*

"Friday March 21 1947.—*Having entered the Square Saint-Jacques at 2 minutes to 3, I sit down facing the tower on the Avenue Victoria side.*

"*A few minutes pass. I can't tear my eyes from the tower's summit until the moment I see blood there.*

"*That's when I make out a man coming towards me (we're the only ones in the garden). No: he walks right by. Stops a little farther on. Retraces his steps. Looks at me. His eyes a strange blue,—humid. He sits down, speaks,* uses the familiar 'tu' form with me. *(My neck, in the vertebral area, had turned to stone and my temples were buzzing.) His age, his voice, indefinable.*

"*Amazing.—Attention, reflection, logic are nothing to me. I no longer am in possession of myself. I am, completely.*

"*But in the course of the conversation this phrase, more sonorous than the others: 'I don't love. I can't love men or women.' (Afterwards I thought of those lively dialogues on the outskirts of sleep which we can sometimes salvage a shred of.)*

"*Then came the rain. He stood up. We walked a little ways together and took the metro, all the while talking about the weather, about the rebirth of spring, about life in Paris. At the entrance to the Tuileries we split up.*

"*38, Rue Saint-X, that's the address he left me, not without giving me a minute description of the staircase of the building and of the room he lived in on the seventh floor.*

"*(If he could be believed, it was a mysterious and irresistible force that led him that day to the Saint-Jacques Tower, since he said he never went out and I could knock on his door any day, any time.)*

"Not long after that, possessed by a warning in a dream, I decided to present myself at the spot he'd mentioned.

"In every detail the interior of the building was as he'd said but both his name and his description were completely unfamiliar to the concierge and the tenants.

"Everything dictated that he remain for me the unknown man."

You can imagine how this narrative was able to reawaken the exaltation that the Saint-Jacques Tower has produced in me for quite some time and which several of my earlier writings or remarks bear witness to. It's certainly true that my mind has often prowled around that tower, for me very powerfully charged with occult significance, either because it shares in the doubly-veiled life (once because it disappeared, leaving behind it this giant trophy, and again because it embodied, as nothing else has, the sagacity of the hermeticists) of the Church Saint-Jacques de la Boucherie, or because it is endowed with legends about Flamel returning to Paris after his death. (It wouldn't take much more than this for the "Completely Black Man," formerly sighted at one of the charnel houses of the Cemetery of the Innocents, and in whose person alchemists recognized the Crow who must be beheaded, to lend Jacques Halpern's interlocutor an even more hallucinatory quality.) It always turns out that my many attempts to enter it, while stalking some improbable find, prove in vain.

That Sunday, April 27, very quickly had no alternative but to settle for less. Besides, the weather was very beautiful and too bright: the uncanny, in any case, would have slipped away. The air wasn't even heavy around the statue of Pascal (whose experiences on this point nevertheless confirm those of Torricelli). A weather station vegetated miserably above his head.

The top of the edifice, where the restoration only spared, I believe, the northern gargoyle, at least revealed a superb glimpse of a Paris in some sense theoretical and outside of time. There, with my bird's-eye view, while I swooped into the touching pearl color of the rooftops, nothing held my attention like the dissimilar life of the arteries which run from the Temple to the Marais, with their idlers of every Sunday past and to come, quite tolerable at this distance, and, no less immemorial, the little precise and schematic game of prostitution in the bright corners of the picture.

I heard, with Apollinaire's ear, the bells of Saint-Merry's ringing.

. . . .

The next evening, April 22, while Hérold was going over in my presence the dedication with which I decorated his copy of my poem Ode to Charles Fourier, *he solicited from me an explanation of a phrase he found in it. In question was a half-joking, half-poetic commentary I placed after one of Fourier's phrases which goes as follows:* "Isocrates *sang the praises of* Busiris . . .; Cardan, *of* Nero . . .; Heinsius, *of* Lice . . .; Majorragius, *of* Mud . . .; Homer, *of* Frogs and Rats . . .; Passerat, *of Nothing . . .;* Lafare, *of Laziness.*"[1]

"This existentialist Passerat," I had added, "never reached us. The Marquis de La Fare arrives with gees on his index finger." Hérold wanted to know what I meant by this bird. I answered him that it was purely the transposition (by homonymic approximation) of the letter G, missing in La Fare, in order to substitute Lafargue, better known and undoubtedly more deserving this as the author of one The Right to Be Lazy *(it's true that my semi-automatic phrase forgot to take into account the U which follows the G.) The above-mentioned commentary, though some might find it extravagant, also served as a leader for the dedication proper: "To Véra and Jacques Hérold, with whom I admired yesterday the 'diamond with a bib' from Australia in the bird market . . ." (after leaving the Saint-Jacques Tower we toured the cages in this market: the one curiosity consisted of a pair of 'diamonds with bibs' whose leaps were quicker than the others and whose plumage, without prejudice to rarer colors which I am now taking pains to arrange, were dominated by the sunlit gray of the rooftops my eye had caressed one moment before, with a black violet petal on its song spot. I don't think I'm straying into a digression if I stress that, concerning this 'diamond,' Hérold's preoccupations in the visual arts are centered, as with no one else*

1 Charles Fourier: *Traité de l'Association domestique-agricole.*

before, on crystal and, concerning the Ode, *that Véra Hérold,—I only learned this from her the next day—had agreed to give a talk on May 5 on: "Fourier the Seer" before the anarchist group of the* X V *th Arrondissement in Paris.)*

I had just finished explaining the *"gees"* when Hérold exhibited complete surprise. He very quickly shared it with me and it will remain among those that count in my life. He then informed me that the day before he'd found himself buying a recently-published work entitled Gérard de Nerval et les doctrines ésotériques[1] *and the frontispiece of the volume was a portrait of Nerval framed in inscriptions from his own hand, certainly tailor-made to astonish me, which he described to me. (But because I've been able to obtain the book since then, just as well to describe the page here* de visu.) *The portrait, once verified, was not unfamiliar to me: it appeared, in fact, but without its border, in Aristide Marie's work:* Gérard de Nerval.[2] *Concerning it, on June 1st, 1854, the poet of the* Chimeras *writes to Georges Bell: "I tremble at the thought of encountering on display a portrait I was made to pose for when I was ill, on the pretext of an obituary. The artist is a talented man, but his work is too true! Spread the word that this is an accurate but posthumous portrait, I want to bathe my face in ambrosia, if the gods will permit me but half a glass." Moreover, the inscriptions, in their totality unpublished to this day, were disquieting in an entirely different way. They consist, in fact, of the following words: at the top border, to the left, "German swan," in the center, "the late G rare," the connection between the letter G and the adjective underlined by a little hyphen. The transition from G to gees, as in my dedication, is clearly indicated, to the right, by the quick sketch of a bird in a cage.[3] Consequently, when it comes to*

---

1   By Jean Richter, Ed. du Griffon d'or, 1947.

2   Librairie Hachette, pub.

3   "Gérard," notes Monsieur Richer, "contrived to learn the 'language of birds,' according to the dictionary of Dupont de Nemours which, however, only encompasses the 'language of crows.'"

this G, I personally cannot help noticing in the portrait the curious position of the index finger meditatively propped on the chin and which, in this plate, falls just below the letter. But I suspect that those familiar with Rimbaud's work will not shudder when they discover at the lower margin, the words, "I am the other," preceded by a question mark and signed with a hexagram with a dot in its center (that's it for the cabalistic signs Aristide Marie insists the portrait is decorated with). The famous "'I' is an other" from the "Letter from a Seer" is thus set back by this blow which nothing led us to expect and poses a problem of sources, *calling for a complete elucidation.*[1]

1   Since these lines were written, in an interval of just a few days, a giant step was taken in this direction, marked by the publication of an essential work entitled *La Symbolique de Rimbaud* (pub. du Vieux Colombier). This work definitively establishes that Eliphas Lévi, whose absolute power over the evolution of Hugo was demonstrated by Monsieur Viatte, exercised a no less preponderant influence on Rimbaud. I held this conviction for a long time and I made a clean breast of it in Haiti in a lecture on the "Occult Origins of Romanticism" (January, 1946) but *La Symbolique de Rimbaud* gives irrefutable proof of it. If I didn't object thoroughly to entering into communication with its author—who revealed himself shortly afterwards to be a young Jesuit—I would attempt to push his research in the direction of my personal line of inquiry; I cannot, under these conditions, even think of it. Since, right after reading his book, which in no way warned me about him, I had initiated that line of inquiry in a dedication to a copy of the *Ode* already cited (I called his attention to the fact that the Abbé Constant, *alias* Eliphas Lévi, had been in close contact with the Phalansterian Bookstore and that in Fourier's case as well, prior to Rimbaud, color symbolism was vigorously affirmed) he answered: "You posed an extremely vast question: 'Must we go back even farther to find the head of the line?' I believe so. Fourier and Lévi are part of an immense current of thought which we can trace to the Zohar and which turns into the Illuminist schools of the XVIIIth and XIXth centuries. We find it again underlying the idealist systems, in Goethe as well and in general in all those who refuse to take mathematical identity as the unifying idea in the world." (May 12, 1947). He was to return to this a week later: "I've just laid my hands on a document you might perhaps know.... Baudelaire wrote to Toussenel, I believe: 'The poet

This work which came to me by such roundabout, such irregular paths (and right after, in a text entitled "In Front of the Curtain,"[1] I had been openly preoccupied with the "phonetic Kabalah") prepared for me, after all, another no less staggering surprise. Just as, at the end of 1940, a long newspaper article inspired by the worst hatred of the time came to warn me that the route given in Paris to the "avengers of the Knights Templar" merged with the one I had unconsciously followed with Nadja, I had, guided by Monsieur Jean Richer's exegesis, no difficulty in convincing myself that here, on the purely symbolic level, I was walking with Nerval along the gilded path. Melusina, Esclarmonde de Foix, the Queen of Sheba, Isis, She Who Pours the Morning, the very beautiful in their order and their oneness will remain for me the safest guarantees.

Eternal youth. "1808=17": Birth of Nerval.—Publication of The Social Destiny of Man; or Theory of the Four Movements.

My only star lives...

Paris, May 1st – 3rd, 1947

---

is *supremely* intelligent, he is *intelligence* par excellence—and imagination is the most *scientific* of faculties because it alone understands the *universal analogy*, or what mystical religion calls *correspondence*. . . .' An idea preoccupies me since I began this book, and that is that you are a true spirit who has strayed into a sect. What, finally, do you owe to Fourier? Nothing, or quite little. Without Fourier you would yet be what you are. *Rational man* did not have to wait for Fourier to arrive on earth in order to understand that nature is a verb, an allegory, a mold, an embossing, if you will. We know that, and it's not from Fourier that we know it: we know it from ourselves and from poets." *(Lettres,* Mercures 1908, p. 83). It goes without saying that for me Baudelaire's opposition to Fourier being above all of a societal nature ("There is no reasonable and secure government but an aristocracy"), cannot, on this point, impress me.

June 1st, 1947

1   *Catalogue de l'Exposition Internationale du Surréalisme,* Galérie Maeght, pub. 1947.

NOTES

PAGE 26: *Arshile Gorky and Agnès Gorky:* Arshile Gorky (1904 – 1948) was a painter who emigrated at a young age from Armenia to the United States. His work derives from Surrealism but is now often seen in the context of Abstract Impressionism, which he greatly influenced. Gorky and Breton were part of a community of expatriate artists who congregated in the northeastern U.S. during World War II.

PAGE 27: Esther *and* Polyeucte: *Esther,* a very chaste tragedy by the French playwright, Racine, written in 1689. *Polyeucte,* a tragedy by Corneille with a Christian theme, written from 1641 – 2.
   Chariots: The Quebec word for bus, *char,* means "chariot" in European French. Breton is finding a kind of home-grown surrealism in the Quebec dialect.

PAGE 28: *Nerval's old Valois:* Gérard de Nerval (1808 – 1855), Romantic poet, grew up in Valois, a historic rural region in north central France. The end of this section puns on the well-known folk song line, *"Alouette, je te plumerai,"*—"Lark, I'll pluck you." Using the name of the tobacco, Breton changes the lyric to "Lark, I'll smoke you."

PAGE 30: *Pré Saint-Gervais:* A suburb northeast of Paris in the industrial belt.

Red flags ... black flags: The red flag is, of course, the symbol of the socialist and communist movements. The black flag is the banner of the anarchists.

PAGE 31: *the Paris Commune:* A rebellion in 1871, considered the first proletarian revolution. It was violently suppressed by the French government.

PAGE 32: NEITHER GOD NOR MASTER: The motto of Auguste Blanqui (1805 – 1881). It was also the name of a paper he edited. Blanqui was a socialist who played a leading role in the formation of the worker's movement in France.

Charonne or Malakoff: Charonne is a district in the eastern part of Paris; Malakoff is a suburb south of Paris.

PAGE 34: *Saint-Simon:* Louis de Rouvroy Saint-Simon (1675 – 1755), a duke who wrote chronicles that were critical of French royalty. Breton apparently read Virgile Josz's words in a work by Saint-Simon. The last year of the reign of Louis XIV was 1715.

PAGE 35: *Watteau:* Antoine Watteau (1684 – 1721), French artist who painted many idealized scenes of lovers courting.

PAGE 38: *"Find the place and the formula":* The last words of Arthur

Rimbaud's prose poem *Vagabonds* in *Illuminations*.

"Possess truth in one soul and one body": The final phrase of Rimbaud's *A Season in Hell*.

PAGE 43: *Grand Grève:* An area between the towns of Gaspé and Percé on the Atlantic coast of Quebec.

PAGE 45: *Paracelsus:* Paracelsus (1493 – 1541) was a German physician who defied academic authorities and dabbled in alchemy. He wrote, "Besides the stars that are established, there is yet another—*Imagination*—that begets a new star and a new heaven."

Sade: Breton probably admired the Marquis de Sade (1740 – 1814) for his challenge to sexual convention and his loyalty to the cause of the French Revolution.

Lautréamont: Isidore Ducasse (1846 – 1870) wrote under the name of Count de Lautréamont. The dream-like imagery in his writing foreshadowed Surrealism.

Marat: Jean-Paul Marat (1743 – 1793), radical leader of the French Revolution. He was the victim of a political assassination.

Saint-Just: Louis de Saint-Just (1767 – 1794). At the age of twenty-six Saint-Just became the leader of France when he was elected president of the ruling body of the French Revolution. He instituted decrees to redistribute property from the nobility to the poor. Saint-Just played a major part in the Reign of Terror and was himself guillotined before his twenty-seventh birthday.

PAGE 47: *Louis* XVI This Louis (1754 – 1793) was the last Bourbon king of France, husband of Marie Antoinette. They were both guillotined during the French Revolution.

PAGE 48: *old men dressed in white:* This vignette and the ones that follow it are semi-mythical episodes about figures in French history, similar to the stories of George Washington chopping down the cherry tree in u.s. political folklore.

the vase of Soissons: Clovis, King of the Franks, plundered a vase from a church after the Battle of Soissons in 486 A.D. When Clovis refused to return the vase, one of his soldiers shattered it. In retaliation, Clovis split the soldier's head.

Philip the Fair (1268 – 1314): French king who quarrelled with Pope Boniface over taxing the clergy. Boniface threatened to embargo French coins sent to Rome. Philip also inflated the currency during his reign.

Charles VI (1368 – 1422): A French king who was intermittently mad in his later years. Legend has it that he saw a stag with a shining cross between his antlers.

Henry III (1551 – 1589): French king who was ultimately killed by forces hostile to his religious policies. His pets were "a small group of handsome young men with whom he indulged in questionable excesses." *(Encyclopedia Britannica)*

Henry IV (1553 – 1610): The king reputed to have said, "Paris is well worth a mass." In the War of the Three Henries, his forces defeated the ultra-Catholic armies led by Charles de Lorraine, Duke of Mayenne. Mayenne is usually portrayed as fat and slow, while Henry's weapon was the speed of his armies.

The Gray Eminence: The original of this phrase was Father François Joseph, Clerk of Tremblay (1577 – 1638), an advisor to Cardinal Richelieu. Richelieu was the Red Eminence; Joseph was his silent partner in French foreign affairs.

PAGE 50: *Charles Fourier* (1772 – 1837): French utopian socialist, whom Breton much admired. He is the subject of Breton's last major poem, *Ode to Charles Fourier,* written just after *Arcanum 17.*

Flora Tristan (1803 – 1844): Early French socialist and feminist, one of the founders of both movements.

Father Enfantin (1796 – 1864): His real name was Barthélemy Prosper Enfantin. He assumed leadership of the Saint-Simon utopian socialist movement after the death of its founder. Though the movement became something of a religious cult under him, Enfantin's writings influenced many socialist activists. He believed that his leadership paved the way for a female messiah who would liberate her sex, and he preached the androgynous nature of divinity.

the customs inspector Rousseau: Henri Rousseau (1844 – 1910), the self-taught artist who painted in a "naive" style. He worked as a customs inspector.

a postman like Cheval: One of the heroes of the Surrealists was Joseph Ferdinand Cheval (1836 – 1924). This postman from the town of Hauterives collected stones on his route and then assembled them in an Ideal Palace embellished with numerous sculptures. He is the subject of Breton's poem, "Cheval the Postman."

PAGE 55: *another rock like a grindstone:* In her book, *André Breton: Hermétisme et Poésie dans Arcane 17,* Suzanne Lamy associates this rock with the philosophers' stone of the alchemists.

old chateaux of Aquitaine . . . the chateau of Montségur, still burning: The chateau of Montségur was seized and dismantled in the 13th century during the purge of the Albigensian Heresy, a belief closely tied to Provençal troubadour love poetry. Troubadours also sang their verses in Aquitaine, the southwestern part of France.

Kleist: Heinrich von Kleist (1777 – 1811), German playwright. A woman he knew with a terminal illness pleaded with Kleist to kill her. He did so, and then shot himself.

Mélisande: The tragic heroine of Maeterlinck's play, *Pelléas et Mélisande,* set to music by Debussy.

PAGE 56: *Peer Gynt:* The Big Curve is a figure in Act II, Scene VII of Henrik Ibsen's fantasy play, *Peer Gynt.* There is much dispute about the meaning of this figure: is it a giant troll or a symbol of the self? The important point here is that Peer Gynt is rescued from this mysterious evil force by powerful women, goaded on by bird voices.

PAGE 59: *Melusina:* The mythical protector of the Chateau of Lusignan, part woman, part serpent. (See Translator's Preface.)

PAGE 60: *that arm of Ingres' Thetis:* From *Jupiter and Thetis,* painted in 1811 by J.A.D. Ingres, in the Musée Granet in Aix-en-Provence. Thetis is kneeling at the foot of Jupiter's throne, reaching up and touching his beard. In Greek mythology, Thetis was a Nereid who tried to resist the advances of Peleus by changing herself into many forms, including a serpent. According to some versions of the story, all seven of her children died when she tried to use fire to make them immortal.

PAGE 61: *extending her arms between those who are about to grapple:* This phrase evokes the painting *The Sabine Women* by Jacques Louis David in the Louvre Museum. Painted in 1799, it shows the Sabine women separating two armed groups—the Romans and the Sabine men—who have come to avenge themselves.

Rémy de Gourmont (1858 – 1915): An essayist and novelist who wrote extensively about the Symbolist poets.

PAGE 62: "change life": From a phrase in Arthur Rimbaud's *A Season in Hell,* Delirium I. The Foolish Virgin wonders if the Infernal Bridegroom "has secrets that can *change life?*"

PAGE 64: *Bilqis:* The Arab name for the Queen of Sheba.

Cleopatra on the morning of Actium: The Battle of Actium, September 2, 31 B.C., marked the defeat of Cleopatra and Mark Antony at the hands of Octavian and the forces of the Roman Senate.

Gustave Moreau's fairy with the griffon: Gustave Moreau (1826 – 1898) was a French Symbolist painter. He executed a few works entitled *Fairy with Griffons* depicting a seated female nude surrounded by mythical beasts. The one Breton probably saw is in the Gustave Moreau Museum in Paris.

PAGE 67: *Hymns to the Night:* A collection of prose poems by Novalis (1772 – 1801), German Romantic writer. This book, published in 1800, was written after the death of his fiancée.

All the magic of night ...: This section is a description of Arcanum 17, the seventeenth card in the Major Arcana of the tarot deck.

PAGE 74: *the Notebooks of the Estates General:* The Estates General comprised the assembly of clergy, nobility, and the people which the kings of France occasionally called into session. When Louis XVI summoned the Estates General in 1789, the delegates set down their grievances against the monarchy in Notebooks. These Notebooks articulated the demands of the coming French Revolution.

the decrees of '93: 1793 marked the most radical period of the French Revolution, when Robespierre and Saint-Just attempted to redistribute wealth through a series of edicts.

the Port-Royal movement: Port-Royal was an abbey of Cistercian nuns near Versailles that became a center of resistance to the Pope and the Jesuits in the mid-17th century. The nuns supported Jansenism, which the Church suppressed along with the Port-Royal abbey.

PAGE 75: *Benjamin Constant* (1767 – 1830): French novelist, essayist, and politician. He is best known for writing the novel *Adolphe.* Constant was a leading opponent of the monarchy in the mid-19th century.

PAGE 75 – 76: *The left-hand stream ... The right-hand stream:* These two streams appear to be the waters issuing from the two vases poured by the female figure in the tarot card, Arcanum 17.

PAGE 82: *the hawk's motionless oar:* The figure of the hawk here seems to suggest Horus, the falcon god of Egyptian mythology. Horus was the son of Osiris and avenger of his father's murder.

PAGE 83: *yet the chest slid down:* This section is a retelling of part of the myth of Osiris (whose corpse is captive in the chest) and Isis (disguised as the "woman at court").

PAGE 87: *Fabre d'Olivet:* Antoine Fabre d'Olivet (1767 – 1825) was a mystic philosopher, poet, and novelist. He was a forerunner of the revival of Provençal language and literature in the 19th century.

PAGE 88: *Eliphas Lévi:* His real name was Alphonse-Louis Constant (1810 – 1875) and Breton sometimes refers to him as the Abbé Constant. In his books Lévi explored two areas of great interest to Breton—utopian socialism and the occult. Lévi also wrote a book called *L'Assomption de la femme ou le Livre de l'amour* which influenced Breton's ideas on women, according to Suzanne Lamy.

PAGE 90: *Populaire:* The French socialist daily newspaper, published from 1918 to 1970.

Pierre Brossolette (1903 – 1944): A hero of the French Resistance. One of the first to join the armed opposition to the Nazis, Brossolette became a political advisor to DeGaulle in 1942. He parachuted several times into occupied zones. Caught by the Germans, he was tortured. To keep from revealing secrets, he killed himself by jumping from a sixth floor window in Gestapo headquarters in Paris.

PAGE 93: *Corday:* Charlotte Corday (1768 – 1793) was from a noble family and opposed the radical turn of the French Revolution. In 1793 she stabbed the revolutionary leader Jean-Paul Marat to death when he was in his bath. She was subsequently guillotined.

Tallien: Jean-Lambert Tallien (1767 – 1820) was the leader of the Thermidorian Reaction which deposed the radical heads of the French Revolution in 1794.

Monsieur Thiers: Adolphe Thiers (1797 – 1877) was a French conservative politician. He headed the government that massacred the rebels of the Paris Commune in 1871.

PAGE 95: *the soldiers of Valmy:* In the Battle of Valmy, fought in northeastern France in 1792, the French army decisively defeated the Prussian invaders who hoped to crush the French Revolution. Goethe, who witnessed the battle, said, "On this spot and on this day begins a new era in the history of the world."

PAGE 96: *the Abbé Constant:* Eliphas Lévi (see note to page 88).

PAGE 101: *Claude de Saint-Martin* (1743 – 1803): French theologian and writer whose works influenced the Romantics.

PAGE 102: *Bacon:* Breton is probably referring to Francis and not Roger Bacon. Roger Bacon (1510 – 1579) had a well-known interest in alchemy, so he would be an interesting figure to Breton. But Francis Bacon (1561 – 1626) called for a rational approach to investigation rather than mere citing of established authority, an idea dear to Breton.

Condillac: Etienne Bonnot de Condillac (1714 – 1780) was a priest who associated with the *Encyclopédistes* of the Enlightenment. He wrote numerous works of philosophy concerning the certainty of sensory perception.

Fourier: See note to page 50.

PAGE 103: *Abel Bonnards:* Abel Bonnard (1883 – 1968) was a poet who became Minister of Education under the pro-Nazi Vichy government.

Giono: Jean Giono (1895 – 1970), a French novelist and poet who was imprisoned twice during World War II—once in 1939 for his pacifism, and again by the Left in 1944 for his alleged sympathy for the fascists.

PAGE 111: *A painter friend of mine:* This could well be Diego Rivera, whom Breton had visited in Mexico.

PAGE 112: *Matta-style Flames:* Referring to the style of the Chilean Surrealist painter, Roberto Matta Echaurren. Matta did several original illustrations for the first French edition of *Arcanum 17.*

PAGE 114: *Apuleius:* Lucius Apuleius (124 – 170 A.D.), Latin writer and philosopher, author of *The Golden Ass,* a book containing legends of metamorphoses.

PAGE 115: *Michelet:* Jules Michelet (1798 – 1874), the most famous of French historians. He also wrote a book on women and one on love.

PAGE 116: *the ibis, the jackal, the vulture, the snake:* In ancient Egypt these animals were all associated with various gods. The ibis was linked with the moon god, Thoth. There is also an ibis in the background of the tarot card, Arcanum 17. Like Osiris, the jackal was an ancient Egyptian god of the dead, under the name Anubis or Wepwawet. In addition, there was an Egyptian cult of the vulture, tied to the deities Nekhebet, Mut, and Neith, also associated with the dead. The crown of the pharaohs had a divine cobra on its front and a number of Egyptian deities were sometimes portrayed as snakes, including Isis and Nephthys.

Nephthys: In Egyptian mythology, she was Osiris' sister and the wife of Seth. With Isis she mourned Osiris' death.

PAGE 117: *the Saint-Jacques Tower:* Breton was intrigued by this Parisian structure and wrote about it in poems and essays. Standing near the Châtelet metro station on the Right Bank, it is the only remnant of the medieval church of Saint-Jacques-la Boucherie, torn down in 1797. The tower is now a weather station.

Jacques Hérold: Born in Romania in 1910, Hérold moved to Paris and became a painter, sculptor, and illustrator in the Surrealist group.

Victor Brauner (1903 – 1966): Born in the same part of Romania as Hérold, Brauner was a painter in the Surrealist movement.

PAGE 119: *Flamel:* Nicolas Flamel (1330 – 1418) was a French writer who was said to have performed the alchemical trick of turning base metals into gold.

Cemetery of the Innocents: The main burial ground of Paris until 1785, when the remains were moved to the Catacombs. It was located right next to what is now the underground shopping mall at Les Halles.

Torricelli: Evangelista Torricelli (1608 – 1647) invented the barometer. The "experiences" of Pascal's statue "confirm" Torricelli's ideas on air pressure.

from the Temple to the Marais: The Quartier du Temple, on the Right Bank, is the area of Paris where, in medieval times, the Knights Templar had their headquarters. Adjacent to it is the Marais, one of Paris' oldest surviving neighborhoods. When Breton wrote this the Marais, now very chic, was a run-down area.

PAGE 120: *the bells of Saint-Merry:* Saint-Merry is a flamboyant Gothic church near the Saint-Jacques Tower.

Isocrates (436 – 338 B.C.): Athenian writer and educator.

Busiris: An Egyptian king mentioned in Greek mythology. His name is probably a Greek transliteration of "Osiris."

Cardano: Gerolamo Cardano (1501 – 1576), Italian mathematician, doctor, and astrologer.

Heinsius: Daniel Heinsius (1580 – 1655), Dutch classical scholar.

Passerat: Jean Passerat (1534 – 1602): French writer and classicist.

the Marquis de la Fare (1644 – 1712): French poet and memoir writer. His last thirty years were, in fact, given over to laziness.

Lafargue: Breton seems to mean Paul Lafargue (1842 – 1911), Karl Marx's son-in-law. Lafargue carried on the Marxist movement in France, and was unlikely to write an essay in praise of laziness.

gees on his index finger: This is part of an elaborate pun that Breton makes using the first letter of Gérard de Nerval's name (G) and the French word for the bird, 'jay.' In French, the letter 'G' sounds like the word *'geai,'* meaning 'jay.' In addition, the name 'Gérard' in French sounds the same as the phrase that means 'rare jay.'

a pair of 'diamonds with bibs': The real English name for these fowls is "diamond birds" or "pardalotes."

PAGE 121: *the poet of* The Chimeras: Gérard de Nerval published twelve sonnets in 1854 under this title. They are among his best-known poems.

PAGE 123: *She Who Pours the Morning:* Possibly the female figure in the tarot card, Arcanum 17.

The Social Destiny of Man: A work of political theory by Charles Fourier.

My only *star* lives: A play on the line, "My only star is dead" from the well-known sonnet *El Desdichado* by Gérard de Nerval.

ANDRÉ BRETON

Born in Tinchebray, France in 1896, André Breton studied medicine and psychiatry, and was highly influenced by the writings of Sigmund Freud. In the First World War, he served in the medical corps.

Upon returning to Paris, Breton became friends with Paul Valéry and Guillaume Apollinaire, and from 1919 to 1923 associated himself with the Dadaist movement. In that same year, he founded the review *Littérature* with Philippe Soupault and Louis Aragon, and he later collaborated with Soupault on *Les Champs magnétiques (The Magnetic Fields)*, the first example of automatic writing in France.

By 1924, Breton and others broke from Tristan Tzara's Dadaism and founded their own Surrealist movement, heralded by the publication of the *Manifeste du surréalisme (Manifesto of Surrealism)*. The same year Breton published another "automatically" written work, *Poisson soluble* ("Soluble Fish").

In 1928 he published the autobiographical and poetic "fiction," *Nadja* (the title of which is the beginning of the Russian word for hope). The work recounts the "mad love" and search for the subjective other, which would be the hallmarks of several surrealist works. Through this work and others, such as *The Second Manifesto of Surrealism* (published in 1930) and *L'amour fou* (1937; *Mad Love*), Breton's name became synonymous with Surrealism, and he became recognized as the major theoretician and "pope" of the movement.

During this same period Breton became involved with Communism, in part through his admiration for Leon Trotsky. Because of Breton's interest in occultism and experimental art, his ties with the official Communist Party were brief and tenuous.

In the late 1930s Breton traveled to Mexico, where he met Diego Rivera and Trotsky. He visited New York in 1941 and founded the magazine *VVV* with Marcel Duchamp, Max Ernst, and David Hare. In 1942 he delivered a lecture at Yale on Surrealism, and two years later, upon a visit to Gaspé Peninsula in Canada, produced *Arcanum 17*. He continued to produce poetry and theoretical statements until the time of his death in Paris in 1966.

ZACK ROGOW

Zack Rogow was awarded the 1994 PEN/Book-of-the-Month Club Translation Prize for his co-translation of *Earthlight* by André Breton (Sun & Moon Press). He also helped translate *The Dice Cup* by Max Jacob (Sun Press). His most recent book of poems is *A Preview of the Dream*, published by Gull Books. He has worked as a production coordinator of a commercial translation agency and as the Managing Director of The Poetry Center at San Francisco State University.

SUN & MOON CLASSICS

This publication was made possible, in part, through an operational grant from the Andrew W. Mellon Foundation and through contributions from the following individuals:

Charles Altieri (Seattle, Washington)
John Arden (Galway, Ireland)
Jesse Huntley Ausubel (New York, New York)
Dennis Barone (West Hartford, Connecticut)
Jonathan Baumbach (Brooklyn, New York)
Guy Bennett (Los Angeles, California)
Bill Berkson (Bolinas, California)
Steve Benson (Berkeley, California)
Charles Bernstein and Susan Bee (New York, New York)
Dorothy Bilik (Silver Spring, Maryland)
José Camillo Cela (in memorium)
Bill Corbett (Boston, Massachusetts)
Fielding Dawson (New York, New York)
Robert Crosson (Los Angeles, California)
Tina Darragh and P. Inman (Greenbelt, Maryland)
Christopher Dewdney (Toronto, Canada)
George Economou (Norman, Oklahoma)
Elaine Equi and Jerome Sala (New York, New York)
Lawrence Ferlinghetti (San Francisco, California)
Richard Foreman (New York, New York)
Howard N. Fox (Los Angeles, California)
Jerry Fox (Aventura, Florida)
In Memoriam: Rose Fox
Melvyn Freilicher (San Diego, California)
Miro Gavran (Zagreb, Croatia)
Peter Glassgold (Brooklyn, New York)
Barbara Guest (New York, New York)
Perla and Amiram V. Karney (Bel Air, California)
Fred Haines (Los Angeles, California)
Václav Havel (Prague, The Czech Republic)
Fanny Howe (La Jolla, California)
Harold Jaffe (San Diego, California)
Ira S. Jaffe (Albuquerque, New Mexico)
Alex Katz (New York, New York)
Tom LaFarge (New York, New York)
Mary Jane Lafferty (Los Angeles, California)

Michael Lally (Santa Monica, California)
Norman Lavers (Jonesboro, Arkansas)
Jerome Lawrence (Malibu, California)
Stacey Levine (Seattle, Washington)
Herbert Lust (Greenwich, Connecticut)
Norman MacAffee (New York, New York)
Rosemary Macchiavelli (Washington, DC)
Beatrice Manley (Los Angeles, California)
Martin Nakell (Los Angeles, California)
Toby Olson (Philadelphia, Pennsylvania)
Maggie O'Sullivan (Hebden Bridge, England)
Rochelle Owens (Norman, Oklahoma)
Marjorie and Joseph Perloff (Pacific Palisades, California)
Dennis Phillips (Los Angeles, California)
Carl Rakosi (San Francisco, California)
David Reed (New York, New York)
Ishmael Reed (Oakland, California)
Janet Rodney (Santa Fe, New Mexico)
Joe Ross (Washington, DC)
Dr. Marvin and Ruth Sackner (Miami Beach, Florida)
Floyd Salas (Berkeley, California)
Tom Savage (New York, New York)
Leslie Scalapino (Oakland, California)
James Sherry (New York, New York)
Aaron Shurin (San Francisco, California)
Charles Simic (Strafford, New Hampshire)
Gilbert Sorrentino (Stanford, California)
Catharine R. Stimpson (Staten Island, New York)
John Taggart (Newburg, Pennsylvania)
Nathaniel Tarn (Tesuque, New Mexico)
Fiona Templeton (New York, New York)
Mitch Tuchman (Los Angeles, California)
Hannah Walker and Ceacil Eisner (Orlando, Florida)
Wendy Walker (New York, New York)
Anne Walter (Carnac, France)
Arnold Wesker (Hay on Wye, England)

If you would like to be a contributor to this series, please send your tax-deductible contribution to The Contemporary Arts Educational Project, Inc., a non-profit corporation, 6026 Wilshire Boulevard,Los Angeles, California 90036.

RECENT BOOKS IN THE SUN & MOON CLASSICS

Also available by André Breton from Sun & Moon Press:

Earthlight

Translated from the French by Bill Zavatsky and Zack
  Rogow,
With a Translator's Preface by Bill Zavatsky

Winner of the PEN/Book-of-the-Month Club Trans-
  lation Prize

Written to friends and fellow Surrealists such as Pablo Picasso, André
Derain, Robert Desnos, Francis Picabia, Pierre Reverdy, and Max
Ernst, the poems in this collection date from 1919 to 1936, spanning
Breton's involvement with Dadaism and his founding and develop-
ment of Surrealism. The range of poetic forms, from the early col-
lage compositions to the "Five Dreams" of *Earthlight* and the incan-
tatory, feverish love poem "Free Union," reveal Breton's composi-
tional methods and styles.

Earthlight stands as an exciting opportunity for American readers
to experience the poetic revolution of Breton's Surrealism, and to be
electrified by his amazing, hallucinatory imagery. This is a poetry
that delivers the "world in a kiss."

"'Five Dreams' and the extended hallucinatory love poem 'Free
Union' demonstrate the deepest workings of a profoundly subver-
sive poetic mind. It was a mind dedicated to the principle that art is
not a mirror held up to life, but a looking-glass whose image we, like
Alice, must always challenge and step through into a higher, more
truly human reality."—*Vancouver Sun*